J. P Austin

The Blue and the Gray

Sketches of a Portion of the Unwritten History of the Great American Civil War

J. P Austin

The Blue and the Gray
Sketches of a Portion of the Unwritten History of the Great American Civil War

ISBN/EAN: 9783337180065

Printed in Europe, USA, Canada, Australia, Japan

Cover: Foto ©ninafisch / pixelio.de

More available books at **www.hansebooks.com**

THE BLUE AND THE GRAY

SKETCHES OF A PORTION OF THE UNWRITTEN HISTORY

OF THE

GREAT AMERICAN CIVIL WAR

A TRUTHFUL NARRATIVE OF ADVENTURE
WITH THRILLING REMINISCENCES OF
THE GREAT STRUGGLE

ON

LAND AND SEA

By J. P. AUSTIN,
Of the Ninth Kentucky Cavalry, C. S. A.

ATLANTA, GA.:
The Franklin Printing and Publishing Co.
1899.

PREFACE.

The author of this little volume, having served in the Confederate army from the inception of the war till its close, covering the area from the Rio Grande to the Atlantic, and from the Gulf to Virginia's southern line, is in possession of many facts and reminiscences which have escaped the notice of former writers when making up their pen-pictures of the great Civil War, and which will furnish important and interesting data for the future historian, when a true and impartial record of the gigantic struggle shall be written.

At the earnest solicitation of many friends the writer has been induced to present these sketches in book form. In doing so, he has tried to avoid anything sectional. That feeling has long since or should have passed away. Whatever tinge of bitterness may have existed between the soldiers of either army has all been forgotten and forgiven by them. The old soldiers of both contendng forces meet, mix and mingle at their annual reunions, and there exchange friendly greetings. Once a year they gather, "the Blue" and "the Gray," around the sacred mounds of their heroic dead, and, with bowed heads and hands, clasped in brotherly friendship, spread garlands on the graves of their departed comrades.

This book is not written by a General, to cover up his blunders or underrate his rivals; it is simply a plain, unvarnished statement of facts as they occurred under the immediate observation of the writer, during the four long and bloody years of "The War Between the States."

The author has avoided minute details of great battles in which he took a part, simply giving the forces employed and the results.

In launching this little bark upon the broad ocean of literature no attempt at literary merit is claimed, fully confident that a generous public will pass over its defects, and, if the time occupied in its perusal should prove interesting and profitable to the reader, the author will feel amply compensated for the time spent in its preparation.

J. P. AUSTIN,
9th Kentucky Cavalry, C. S. A.

INDEX.

CHAPTER VI.

CHAPTER VII.

CHAPTER VIII.

CHAPTER IX.

CHAPTER X.

CHAPTER XI.

CHAPTER XII.

CHAPTER XIII.

CHAPTER XIV.

CHAPTER XV.

Appendix.

THE BLUE AND THE GRAY.

CHAPTER I.

CHARACTER OF SETTLERS OF THE COLONIES, NORTH AND SOUTH—PRESIDENTS AND ISSUES UP TO 1861—THE NORTHERN PEOPLE THE ORIGINAL DIS-UNIONISTS—WHAT LED TO THE WAR BETWEEN THE STATES.

New England was settled by the Puritans, who effected the revolution of 1620, and decapitated Charles I.

On the contrary the Southern Colonies were occupied by a more loyal class. To the noble family of Baltimore was granted, by royal charter, the province of Maryland. To other staunch adherents of the crown were ceded grants and privileges in Virginia, North and South Carolina, and Georgia.

George Washington was the first Federal magistrate. During his term the people divided into two hostile parties, each striving for office, through the profession of opposite principles.

The New England States, led by John Adams, advocated the power of the Federal Government, even to the straining of the Constitution. This was the Federal party. The Southern States, led by Thomas Jefferson, maintained the rights of the States against the Federal encroachments. This was the Democratic party.

In 1797 John Adams, of Massachusetts, was

elected President. During his term the "alien and sedition" laws were passed by the Federal Congress. These enactments were opposed by the statesmen of the South, since, in their opinions, they invested the Executive with powers not conferred by the Constitution, inimical to popular rights.

The creation of a national bank was also a subject of keen controversy. The public men of the North sustained it with energy, while those of the South opposed it as unconstitutional and of doubtful expediency.

In 1801 Thomas Jefferson, of Virginia, was elected President. During his term the New England States showed a bitter animosity toward the South, which arose, chiefly, from the South's having put a limit to the slave-trade, in which those States were profitably engaged. Therefore, when President Jefferson proposed the purchase of Louisiana from France, the Eastern States violently resisted, because it increased the power and territory of the South.

In 1805 Thomas Jefferson was re-elected to the Presidency. His second term was troubled by the war between England and France. The Berlin and Milan decrees of Napoleon, and the orders in council of the British Government, equally assailed American interests. Our vessels, bound either to English or French ports, incurred the danger of capture and confiscation. This left but one alternative, either to abandon our trade with Europe or go to war to protect it. To escape the latter Mr. Jefferson recommended an " Embargo Act," to put a temporary stop to all foreign trade. This was vehemently opposed by the New England States, because their interests, being chiefly commercial, were seriously damaged. The "Embargo Act" was passed by Congress in December, 1807, whereupon the Eastern States threatened to secede from the Union and form a Northern Confederacy. It will thus be seen that they first recognized the right of a State to secede from the Union and to declare their purpose to carry it into practical effect.

In 1809 James Madison, of Virginia, was elected President. It was during his administration, May, 1812, that Congress declared war against Great Britain.

In 1813 James Madison was re-elected President. During the war the government was supported by direct taxes and requisitions upon the States. The New England States refused, for the most part, to contribute, thus again declaring State sovereignty.

In 1817 James Monroe, of Virginia, was elected President. During his term the interests of the country prospered; no struggle occurred between the politicians of New England and those of the South until 1820, when Missouri applied for admission into the Union as a slave-state. The Eastern States opposed it violently, on the ground that it would be extending slave-territory. The Union was in danger of dissolution.

In 1821 James Monroe was re-elected President. During this term a new conflict arose between New England and the South, on the subject of the tariff. New England demanded more protection; the South opposed it.

In 1825 John Quincy Adams, of Massachusetts, was elected President. During this term a heated contest was carried on between New England and the South on the tariff policy.

In 1829 Andrew Jackson, of Tennessee, became President. During this term the extreme tariff policy of New England led to violent remonstrance on the part of South Carolina, whose interests were seriously injured.

In 1833 Andrew Jackson was re-elected President. During this term the national bank question was the issue.

In 1837 Martin Van Buren, of New York, was elected President. During this term great financial disorder prevailed in the country.

In 1841 William Henry Harrison, of Ohio, was elected President. He died about a year after his accession to office, and the Presidency was then administered by the Vice-President, John Tyler, of Virginia. During his term, a new slave-state, Texas, was admitted into the Union.

In 1845 James K. Polk, of Tennessee, was inaugurated President. During this term, the Mexican war was fought, by which the United States acquired a large acquisition to her territory.

In 1849 Zachary Taylor, of Mississippi, became President, but died and was succeeded by Millard Filmore, Vice-President. During this term, the acquisition of new territory afforded the public men of both sections, a fertile field for discussion.

In 1853 Franklin Pierce, of New Hampshire, became President. During his term, the discussion of the slavery question was renewed. A portion of our Western territory (Nebraska) was divided into two territories—one of these Kansas and the other Nebraska. The New England Emigrant Aid Society was organized in 1854, for the purpose of securing emigrants as settlers in Kansas; these men were all armed with Sharp's rifles and Colt's revolvers. These hostile bands and other bands of armed men from the North and East invaded the territory, forcing the Federal Government finally to interfere. The leaders of the anti-slavery *propaganda*, having violated the Federal prerogative by adopting a constitution and establishing the machinery of a State government, were indicted for treason and obliged to take flight.

In 1857, James Buchanan was inaugurated President. The whole of this term was disturbed by a heated contest between the politicians of the North and the South, on the subject of slavery in the territories.

It is worthy of notice in this connection that most of them knew but little of slavery and slaveholders, beyond what they learned from excited, caressed and tempted fugitives, or from a superficial, accidental or prejudiced observation. From distorted facts, gross misrepresentation, and frequently malicious caricatures, they had come to regard Southern slave-holders as the most unprincipled men and women in the universe; with no incentive but avarice; no feeling but selfishness; and no sentiment but cruelty.

In October, 1859, an event occurred which amazed

the whole country. I allude to the invasion of the State of Virginia by John Brown at the head of an armed force. This man Brown had figured in "Bleeding Kansas," as a daring ring-leader of an anti-slavery band that had contested for the mastery there. When these bloody contests subsided, he was reduced to inaction, and he chafed at the loss of the stern excitement congenial to his fierce nature.

Whether it was fanaticism or ambition that inspired him, no one can say. He conceived the horrible project of setting on foot a servile insurrection. Followed by a handful of desperate men, he suddenly entered the State of Virginia, seized the arsenal of the Federal Government, at Harper's Ferry, to obtain the arms they needed; and raised the cry of "Freedom to Slaves." To his astonishment, no doubt, the affrighted blacks ran to their masters for protection. Some were shot while trying to escape. This nefarious attempt was quelled by the arrest of Brown and his confederates; and their subsequent trial and execution.

On the 6th of November, 1860, the long agitation on the slavery question, which began in 1803, ended with the election of Abraham Lincoln, the representative of the Abolition, or Republican party, as President. Then the dreadful banquet of slaughter began, which ended in the destruction of the most magnificent social fabric the world ever saw.   .

CHAPTER II.

When South Carolina went out of the Union I
gave up all hope of any compromise or reconciliation
between the North and the South. At that time I
was a member of the Galveston Artillery, a company
composed of the first young men of the "Island City."
It was commanded by Captain McCloud, an elegant
gentleman and a trained soldier. He was a graduate of the Military Academy at West Point.

Texas, like the rest of the Southern States, on the
inauguration of Mr. Lincoln, in 1861, was thrown
into commotion from center to circumference. Secession was "rampant." War was the cry.

A convention was at once called to meet at the
capital of the State, with a view to taking the State
out of the Union. At the assembling of the convention the ordinance of secession was passed with but
one vote in opposition to the measure, and that came
from ex-Governor Throgmorton.

When the tall form of the ex-governor arose and
he had proclaimed his vote a tumultuous explosion of
hisses greeted him from all parts of the lobby and
thronged galleries, where the beauty and chivalry of
the State had gathered to witness the scene of Texas

, severing her connection with the Federal Union, and
assuming her original nationality, under the "Lone
Star," which flag at that time was floating from the
dome of her capitol.

After the confusion had somewhat subsided the
gallant Texan addressed the chair; and turning with
a withering look in the direction from whence the
hisses came, with his arms extended, he proclaimed
in a voice that could be distinctly heard to the re-
motest corner of the hall: "*When patriots weep the
rabble hiss.*" He further stated that since his State
stood isolated and alone, by the action of that convention, as an independent republic, and war was inevitable, he asked how many would join him in her
defense? The ex-governor, to prove his loyalty to
his State, at once commenced raising a regiment.
A more gallant or heroic soldier never marched beneath the "Stars and Bars."

General Sam Houston, that grand old hero, patriot
and statesman, was governor of Texas at the time
the convention assembled. He refused to ratify the
proceedings of the convention, on the ground that he
failed to see that separate State secession would accomplish the object sought; which, after an immense
sacrifice of blood and treasure, alas! proved to be
too true. For this act of supposed disloyalty to
his State, he was deposed as governor. From my
earliest recollections I have entertained an exalted
opinion of General Houston's political views; and,
in justice to the warm friendship that existed between himself and my family, I deem it just and
proper to define, just here, his position in regard to

the question of secession. He loved the old flag, and was warmly attached to its associations. It was a trying hour to the hero of Sanjacinto (the result of which battle gave an empire to the South), to see the banner he loved so well and followed so successfully during the war of 1812, give place to another. He was not alone in his regrets at parting with the old standard, for many felt on that sad occasion that the last cherished hope of perpetuating the Republic had gone. General Houston was in favor of calling a convention of all the States, made up of conservative and patriotic men from both sections—not of demagogues and politicians—then, after a full, fair and open presentation of all matters in dispute, if an amicable adjustment could not be reached, and war was inevitable, let the South take the old flag and the Constitution of the United States and declare for the principles of our fathers. It has been conceded by some of our most thoughtful and sagacious statesmen that, had such a policy been adopted, the result would have been far different; but his voice was not heeded.

When that venerable statesman saw that a collision between the North and the South could not be averted he retired to his plantation, where he remained in quiet repose until just before the war closed, when he died. His name will go down in song and story as one of the most remarkable men, in many respects, this country ever produced.

After the proceedings of the convention were known Texas was all ablaze, and steps were immediately taken to place her on a war footing.

About that time an expedition was organized at
Galveston with eight hundred State troops, under
command of Gen. E. B. Nichols, of Galveston, des-
tined for Brazos Santiago, to capture Fort Brown
and all the other military posts along the Rio Grande.
The Federal troops were being concentrated at Fort
Brown (Brownsville, Texas), by order of Gen.
Twiggs.

I was a member of the Galveston artillery at that
time, which company had offered its services to the
State and had been accepted; and on the 16th day of
March, 1861, the command embarked on board the
steamship "General Rusk," of the Morgan line.

I will here insert an article which appeared in the
Atlanta Constitution several years ago, which was
prompted by an incident which occurred on this
trip, and will explain, without the shadow of a doubt,
the true authorship of the song so popular at the
North during the war, " JOHN BROWN'S BODY LIES
MOLDERING IN THE GROUND":

Judge Robert L. Rogers, the efficient and faithful
Secretary of the Fulton County Confederate Veterans' Association, says the *Constitution*, is daily
acquiring facts that will some day find their way into
the history of the late war.

The judge was in a reminiscent mood, and among
other things said :

" You all know that the famous song concerning
' John Brown's body' is generally a familiar air. It
used to be sung with great force by the soldiers in
our Confederate camps. Since the war it has been a
popular song in the South, often sung in theaters by

minstrel troops to the cheers of crowded houses. The origin of the song and the name of the author or composer of it have recently come to my own understanding in a peculiar way.

"A few days ago I met Colonel J. P. Austin, who related the incidents to me and furnished to me the verifying matter. Colonel Austin was a distinguished soldier in the Confederate service. He served in the famous Texas Rangers. He is of that celebrated family of Austins, who have made a great name in Texas, where he formerly lived. The city of Austin, the capital of Texas, bears its name in honor of the family name. Col. J. P. Austin lives now in this, Fulton county, about five miles south of Atlanta. He has been here a good many years, and has been separated from his regimental comrades ever since the close of the war.

"Advertising may often bring good and pleasant results in other ways besides the special business for which the advertising may be done. A few weeks ago a little piece of newspaper used as wrapping for a small parcel of goods came into the hands of Colonel Austin. Casually looking over it his eye came upon a name which he had not seen nor heard since the war, and yet it seemed at once to be familiar in memory. The name was Theo Noel, and the advertisement was of his business in Chicago as assayer, geologist and metallurgist. Taking the address from that, Colonel Austin resolved to write to him to inquire if he was the same Theo Noel who soldiered with him during the war. He remembered one by such name, but had had no tidings of him since the war.

"A few days ago a reply came. With it came a clipping from the *Chicago Tribune.* Here are both the reply of Mr. Noel to Colonel Austin and the clipping reciting the facts concerning the song of 'John Brown's Body.'"

The letter from Mr. Noel to Colonel Austin reads:

" CHICAGO, June 1.—Colonel J. P. Austin, South Atlanta, Ga.:   My Dear Sir and Old Comrade:— Your letter of the 29th ultimo found its way to my desk, where, upon an average, only one in a hundred reach. You have located me aright.   I was one of the Davis Guard, and went from Galveston with you on the old steamer Rusk, and afterwards served in your company for six months as a Texas Ranger.

" I enclose you herewith a letter I wrote to the *Chicago Tribune*, which will explain itself, but which I want you to return to me, for it is the only one that I have left.   This letter was published in many other papers.

" I have been away from Texas for twenty-two years.   My home has been in Chicago.   While operating in the mines of the Northwest I struck V. O., and I am no longer a miner.   I was in Texas last February for the first time in eighteen years.   The enclosed will explain all to you on that score, and show you what I was doing there.

" In San Antonio I met old Colonel ' Rip ' Ford, who looks just as he did when he called us up on our first parade in old Fort Brown, when, as you will remember, the Mexican bands were playing their national tunes on the opposite bank, while we, poor devils of rebels, were standing under the Lone Star flag, not even dipping our banners or presenting arms to the three steamer loads of United States soldiers passing by to the tune of ' Star-spangled Banner.'   I often recall this scene and think how the last one of us devils should have been sunk in the bottom of the ocean for driving from our land that band of patriots, and trampling on the old flag our fathers and forefathers made.

" Well, old comrade, now that we have met, so to speak, I wish to hear from you again, and shall surely

esteem it the greatest pleasure of my life to have
you come and see me here in Chicago, as many of
my old comrades have. I know that we could spend
a week or more recalling our war experiences, as I
also know it would be a great pleasure to us both.

"When you go to Atlanta again call on my old
friend, Rev. Sam Small, who has often visited me in
Chicago, and with whom I was connected down in
Texas for some years, and who is a personal friend
of mine. Show him the enclosed letter which I
wrote to the *Chicago Tribune*, and tell him I want
it reproduced in the *Atlanta Constitution*.

"On the 30th ultimo I received from the ladies of
Texas sixteen boxes and baskets of flowers, which
were scattered over the graves of the 7,000 Confederate soldiers buried at Oakwoods, who died at Camp
Douglass, in this city, and where, with about five or
six ex-Confederates in this city, we have erected a
grand monument.

"Hoping to hear from you again and often, I am,
sir, yours truly,

"THEO NOEL."

The clipping from the *Chicago Tribune* to which
Mr. Noel referred, was:

"JOHN BROWN'S BODY," COMPOSED ORIGINALLY BY
A REBEL.

"CHICAGO, September 21.—Editor *Tribune:*

"The lines, 'John Brown's body lies moldering
in the tomb, But his soul goes marching on,' etc.,
were composed, written and sung by Charley Rees,
private in the Davis Guard, on board the steamer
General Rusk, on the 16th day of March, 1861, between Galveston and Brazos Santiago. Seven hundred and fifty Texas Rangers, made up in Galveston,
forming a part of General MacLeod's expedition
from Galveston to take the Rio Grande forts and the

United States troops that had been concentrated at
Fort Brown, Brownsville, Tex., by order of General
Twiggs, were placed on the Harris & Morgan
Steamer, General Rusk.   While on the way speech-
making was the order of the day, and, if I mistake
not, it was Captain Austin, a descendant of the original Texas Austins, who said in substance :   ' Yes, it
is true, we have hung the inciter of insurrection, and
his body lies moldering in the ground, but let me
tell you his accursed spirit and soul marches on, and
unless we meet as becomes brave men, the abolition
hordes will,' etc.   Whereupon the lines above were
written by Rees.

" What has become of Rees I know not, but this
I do know, that, after serving with him for six
months at Fort Brown, the day we were mustered
out, September 10, 1861, by Colonel John S. Ford
('Old Rip,' as the Rangers called him), Rees showed
me the John Brown song, sent to him by a relative,
I think in Jersey City, rewritten and paraphrased to
do service in Northern camps, and the words, ' We'll
hang Jeff. Davis,' etc., added.   If I am not mistaken
Rees went to Matamoras, Mexico, and from there
came North.   I write from a personal knowledge of
the facts, for I was there.   Yours truly,
                                    " THEO NOEL."

On reaching Brazos Santiago, our command at
once took up its line of march for Brownsville, opposite the city of Matamoras.   On the route we passed
over the historic battle-fields of " Resaca de la
Palma," and " Palo Alto," where American valor
achieved imperishable renown, in days that were
past, under the command of General Taylor, whose
name will ever stand conspicuous on the pages of
our country's history.

On reaching Brownsville our command was re-organized, for six months' service, under Colonel John S. Ford—" Old Rip," the boys called him.

He was a noted Indian fighter, and a typical frontiersman.

Brownsville is a beautiful little town, situated on the banks of the classic Rio Grande, just opposite the Mexican city, Matamoras. We found the town astir with United States troops, making preparations for their departure. They were a jolly set of fellows, and it was indeed lamentable to think that so soon we were to be arrayed against each other in bloody conflict.

CHAPTER III.

LIFE AT BROWNSVILLE—AN OLD FRIEND—A MEX-
ICAN BEAUTY—FEDERALS LEAVE—AN AFFAIR
OF HONOR—WE LEAVE BROWNSVILLE.

I will here relate an incident which may have a
slight tinge of romance. It will crop out at intervals, as these sketches progress. Every feature of it
is based upon facts. As the parties most conspicuous in this episode are now living, I have deemed it
best to withold their names; but they will recognize
and acknowledge the correctness.

On reaching Brownsville, I chanced to meet with
an old friend, a young artillery officer of the regular
army. We had met before, in years past, on the
frontier of Texas, and had slept under the same
blanket; toasted our meat by the same camp-fire, and a
warm attachment had sprung up between us. Imag-
ine my surprise at meeting him under such circumstances. As he grasped my hand, he seemed to hesitate, as if reflecting on the past. Was it possible
that we were to be arrayed against each other in the
bloody strife so near at hand?

He remarked, "Go, do your duty, Captain; I shall
try to do mine. It is useless for us to discuss the issues that brought on this war. Although Southern
born, I can never abandon the old flag."

My friend was a native of Kentucky, and a graduate of West Point. He was handsome, brave and
courteous. He had the gentlemanly bearing that

education, gentle blood and associations alone can furnish. He was tall, graceful, and of commanding appearance; and his genial spirit, affable and courteous address, at once revealed the thorough mental and physical training he had received at the United States Military Academy. In fact, he was a cultured gentleman, and as magnificent a specimen of American manhood as one would meet with in a lifetime. My young friend was not long in choosing which side he would take in this great struggle. Coming from revolutionary stock and cherishing a strong veneration for the old flag of our fathers, he cast his fortunes on the side of the Union.

The United States troops remained but a few days after our arrival in Brownsville, but it was my good fortune to spend much of that time with my friend.

His natural disposition was lively and cheerful, but at times I could discover what I thought to be a sad expression mantling his manly face.

On the evening previous to his departure, while we were taking a stroll along the banks of the river, I noticed an unusual depression in his general bearing, and requested an explanation.

"Yes," said he, "I feel somewhat depressed just at this time;" and then confided to me his secret.

"Do you see yonder villa, on the opposite side of the river, nestling beneath the shade of a beautiful live-oak grove, with long festoons of Spanish moss drooping gracefully from their branches? Within the walls of that charming abode, dwells the idol of my heart's adoration.

2 b g

" Captain, you will please pardon my seeming melancholy, when I suffer my mind to reflect upon the thought that I am so soon to gaze into the liquid depths of those dark eyes, perhaps, for the last time."

"Lieutenant you excite my curiosity. I must know more about this matter," I replied.

" Very well," said he, as he consulted a handsome gold chronometer, which he drew from his fob, and requested me to meet him at the ferry at half-past six, and he would be pleased to have me call with him at the cozy little retreat above mentioned.

By this time we had reached our quarters, where we separated to make the necessary preparations for our visit. At the appointed time we met on the river bank. The lieutenant was in full dress uniform, and I thought he was the most graceful and fascinating military officer I had ever seen.

" We crossed the river on a ferry boat, and wended our way to the charming abode of the fair one, some half a mile in the distance where we presented our cards and were ushered into an elegantly furnished drawing-room, in all the appointments of which was an indication of the refinement and wealth of the occupants. In due time the young beauty presented herself; her gentle courtesy, pleasant and refined deportment, at once made the impression on my mind that we were in the presence of one of Mexico's fairest and most cultivated daughters. She was the daughter of a wealthy Spaniard, who held a conspicuous position in the government. She had received all the advantages that an ample fortune, travel and an indulgent parent could bestow. Her voice, with its sweet Southern accent, was as soft and mellow as the wind that sighed through the rich foliage at her latticed window.

Her well-developed form and the perfect symmetry of her features at once stamped her as a child of gentle birth:

> "And ne'er did Grecian chisel trace
> A nymph, a Naiad, or a Grace,
> Of finer form, or lovelier face."

In the liquid depths of her dark eyes could be traced the fires of a noble intellect. The evening was spent in a delightful manner, interspersed with music and other amusements incident on such occasions. As the conversation would become animated those melting orbs would send forth flashes that were in unison with the glittering gem that sparkled at her throat.

It did not require a close observer, in the presence of this dark-eyed señorita and the gallant young officer, to discover that there were "two minds with but a single thought; two hearts that beat as one."

Both seemed to avoid alluding to the separation which was so soon to take place—

> "Which might be for years, and it might be forever."

As we bade the young charmer adieu for the night I noticed a treacherous tear moistening her glowing cheek, unobserved, however, by him whose bosom was heaving with tender emotions.

> "The rose is fairest when 'tis budding new,
> And hope is brightest when it dawns from fears;
> The rose is sweetest washed with morning dew,
> And love is loveliest when embalmed in tears."

It took but a few days to make the necessary prepa-

rations for the departure of the Federal troops from
Brownsville to Point Isabel, at the mouth of the Rio
Grande, from whence they were to take shipping for
the North.   It was about noon when I shook hands
with my gallant young friend, as he stepped on board
the boat which was to convey him down the river
with his fellow officers.   As he bade me "good-bye"
he remarked : " Captain, should we chance to meet
on the battle-field and recognize each other, elevate
your gun, and I will do the same." We both nodded
assent, and the little steamer was soon puffing away
down the river.   Just then might have been seen a
delicate, white scarf fluttering from the balcony of a
distant hacienda on the opposite side of the river, almost obscured by the dense foliage of a cluster of live-
oaks.   The response was given from the pilot-house
of the little steamer, as she rounded the bend of the
river, and was lost to view.   This last exchange of
signals had no doubt been previously agreed upon.
It is easy to suppose that the withdrawal of the snowy
pennant from the window was accompanied by a sigh
from that fair tropical flower, as she took a last look
at the fast-receding form of the object upon whom
the purest and holiest sentiments of her heart were
centered, every throb of which struck a responsive
chord in the breast of the young officer of artillery,
who, with his companions, was hastening afar to
scenes of carnage, blood and strife.

The monotonous hum-drum of garrison duty while
at Brownsville would be, at this time, of very little
interest to the general reader. We passed through all
the features incident to such a life, such as drawing

rations, drilling, guard mount and dress parade. A little affair of honor took place which relieved the monotony while there, which I will relate, as it is closely connected with one of the principal characters previously mentioned.

Three or four weeks after the departure of the United States troops a young Englishman arrived in the city of Matamoras. He was a regular dude, with mutton-chop whiskers and hair parted in the middle. He represented himself as Duke, Count, or Lord, I disremember which. He brought letters of introduction to some of the prominent men of the city; soon made himself quite conspicuous by his extremely English ways, and moved in the first circles of society. He was not long in forming the acquaintance of our fair young heroine, and as a natural consequence became desperately smitten, for but few could resist her charms. He pressed his suit with alacrity and vigor. She received his attentions with that refined and gentle courtesy so characteristic of her nature. At the home of the young lady was a young gentleman, a cousin, on a visit from the City of Mexico. He was handsome, refined and intelligent; every move and feature indicated his pure Castilian blood. He did not take kindly to the Englishman; he thought his attentions to his fair cousin, at times, assumed the character of rudeness. Upon one occasion he remarked, in the presence of a party of gentlemen, that he thought " the Englishman was an adventurer hunting for a fortune." These remarks reached the ears of "John Bull," who was highly indignant; so much so that he sent the Spaniard his card. A

challenge passed and was accepted.   Pistols at ten
paces (without " coffee ") was the result.   The place
of meeting was three miles above the city, on the
bank of the river and in a beautiful grove.   On the
morning designated the principals, with their seconds,
drove out in carriages to the ground, where both were
promptly on time.   The preliminaries were soon
arranged, and the two antagonists placed in position.

They cast a glance of cool determination at each
other; the word was given, and at the discharge of
the weapons, which seemed almost simultaneous, the
Englishman fell forward and was caught by his
second.   The surgeon in attendance at once exam-
ined the wound.   It was very painful, but was not
considered fatal.   He recovered in a few weeks, and
was not long in deciding that the frontier was no
place for an " Hinglishman."   The border was a little too rough for his sensitive nature; so the Brit-
isher packed his grip and struck out far across the
water, carrying with him a substantial reminder of
his eventful career in the " Wild West."   His antagonist had left some time before for his home in
the City of Mexico.

Thus ended this affair of honor, with the warm,
impulsive blood of the South on the one side, and the
stern, inflexible will of the North on the other.

After the affair just narrated I saw but little of the
fair charmer who was the innocent cause of the hostile meeting.   The vibrations of her mellow voice,
accompanied by her delicate touch on her instrument,
could sometimes be heard on a moonlight night, as

the soft, summer winds wafted the sweet strains of some favorite song through her latticed window.

A few weeks previous to our departure from Brownsville I received a note from the young lady, requesting me to call at her home, as she had some important information she wished to convey.

It was just at dusk when I received the message, and I hastened to make the necessary preparations to comply with her request. On reaching her home I found her seated in a beautiful bower, beneath a grove of magnolias, with a cluster of rare tropical flowers in her hand. All were evidences of her refined and elegant taste. As she arose and extended her hand, and I saw the animated expression of those dark eyes, I thought I had never seen anything half so lovely, and so expressed myself. With a gentle bow, a delicate tinge for a moment mantled her glowing cheek, she offered me a seat by her side, and at once informed me that she had received a letter from Lieutenant ————. It had traveled a circuitous route before reaching her. I did not inquire as to the tender messages it contained; I was only interested about the locality of my friend. At the time he wrote he was in Washington City, but had just been ordered to report to the Army of the Cumberland.

General Grant was concentrating at the time a large force in the vicinity of Nashville, Tenn., and letters could only be transmitted to the United States through Mexico at that time.

I will now bid adieu to my fair young friend until

I again make a bow to her under far different circumstances.

Our term of service having expired, we commenced making preparations to depart for Galveston. We had made many friends while stationed at Brownsville, and left them with regret. We were paid off in " Texas Scrip," which we were compelled to dispose of at a heavy discount.

Most of the boys returned to their homes in different parts of the State and enlisted in the Confederate service. The writer, with a few friends, went across the country on horseback.

CHAPTER IV.

RETURN TO GALVESTON—CAPTURE OF CAPTAIN
CHUBB AND HIS CREW—THEIR TRIAL AND
DEATH-SENTENCE—MR. DAVIS GIVES MR. LIN-
COLN NOTICE AND PREPARES FOR RETALIATION
—CHUBB AND HIS MEN RELEASED—RECRUITING
—CARTER'S BRIGADE.

On reaching our old stamping ground we found
that great changes had taken place since we left, six
months before. The busy marts of trade in the Island
City had become depositories for army stores; and the
sound of marching squadrons greeted the ear at every
turn. The beautiful "City by the Sea" was shut out
from all intercourse with the outside world on the
water side, a squadron of United States warships having blockaded her port. Nothing daunted, Texas
was making preparations for whatever might occur.

Sumter had fallen, and the first great battle of the
war, which resulted in a complete victory for the
South, had been fought.

Previous to the attack on Fort Sumter there was a
strong Union sentiment in the South, and thousands
cherished the hope that war might be averted; but
their vague anticipations, like the school-boy's dream,
was never to be realized. About this time an incident
occurred which I have never seen in print, and which
will go to show the vigilance of the blockaders.

A patrol force, consisting of about thirty men, all
experienced seamen, had been organized at Galveston
to watch the movements of the Federal warships, as

there were strong indications that a night attack might be made on the city. Captain Thomas Chubb, a native of Boston, Mass., a retired sea captain, and for a long time a pilot on Galveston bar, was placed in command of the squad. Every night a boat was stationed just inside the bar to watch the maneuvers of the fleet. On the night in question Captain Chubb, with a select crew of seven men, took their station. They were sighted from the deck of one of the ships, and a scheme was put on foot to capture them. The night was very dark; about 12 o'clock a launch with muffled oars, put off from one of the ships on its silent mission. It pulled alongside the guard-boat unobserved, and succeeded in capturing the whole party without a struggle. It was discovered early next morning that something had gone wrong with Captain Chubb and his party, and a flag of truce was sent out to ascertain their fate, when it was learned that they had been captured, placed in irons and stowed away in the hold of the vessel.

The commander did not see proper to treat them as prisoners of war; to which a strong protest was made by the commander of the Confederate forces at Galveston. The prisoners were taken to Philadelphia, where they were placed on trial for their lives, high treason being the charge. They were found guilty and sentenced to be hanged within a month; hardly time for an "Old Salt" to shape his matters up for so long a cruise.

As soon as their fate was made known at Richmond Mr. Davis selected an equal number of prominent prisoners, among whom was a member of Congress by the name of Cochran, who went out to witness the first battle of Manassas. Mr. Davis sent a communication to President Lincoln informing him that on the very same day and hour that those Confederate prisoners were executed, he would retaliate by having the men he had designated " swung." This was something the Federals were not prepared for, and caused a halt. They decided to look a little further into the matter; the result of which was the Confederates were to be held as prisoners of war. It was a close call, however, and had it not been for the prompt action of Mr. Davis eight of our gallant heroes might have " looked up a rope."

In a few weeks after the above our men were exchanged, and all reached their homes in safety. Captain Chubb was the hero of the hour. He was received with open arms by his friends and with showers of congratulations for the fortunate escape he and his companions had made from the terrible fate that overhung them.

Captain Chubb was a " red-hot " secessionist from the start, and would often afterwards relate to his friends in that positive and emphatic manner, so characteristic of the man, his feelings on that memorable day when he was ordered to stand up and receive his sentence of death. He would often say that whenever he thought of it it would produce a peculiar itching sensation about the throat. He was to the day of his death a staunch friend of Jefferson Davis. As has been stated, he was a native of Boston, but was often heard to remark, that it was a good place to be born in if you only left it in time.

Recruiting was going on rapidly, all over the State. All classes of people were drifting to the army. Three noted regiments were raised about this time in middle Texas, which constituted Carter's brigade; a brief account of which I deem not out of place in these sketches. These regiments were composed of gentlemen, mostly planters, and the best blood of the State. The colonels were George W. Carter, Frank C. Wilkes, and C. C. Gillespie, all Methodist ministers, who left the sacred desk, to take service under the "Stars and Bars."

Carter's brigade did gallant service in Louisiana, Texas, and Arkansas. Colonel Carter was a man of versatile talent, having officiated as minister, lawyer, soldier, and journalist, and, withal, he was an accomplished orator. When the war closed Colonel Carter drifted to New Orleans, where he became editor of a "red-hot" Republican paper, and was as enthusiastic in upholding the Federal Reconstruction measures as he was four years previous in raising his regiment for service in the Confederate army. He was soon rewarded by being elected a member of the House of Representatives from Louisiana, and afterwards rose to the speaker's chair. He never again visited Texas, and many of his old comrades believe he died years ago.

Colonel Wilkes was taken prisoner at Arkansas Post. A few months before General Lee's surrender he wrote a letter to a friend in Texas, in which he stated that the war was certain to result in the success of the Federal arms, and giving his reasons. The letter was published in all the Texas papers and created a sensation. The word "traitor" was coupled with his name, but time showed that his predictions were correct, and the very men who denounced him were his best friends when he returned home. He was an efficient officer and a gallant soldier. He died several years ago.

Colonel Gillespie was a "red-hot war man," and commanded a splendid regiment. When the war closed the Colonel became editor of a paper in Houston, Texas, where he "died in harness," during the days of reconstruction.

Thus it was, that Texas, in this famous brigade, furnished as fine a body of men as ever went into the Confederate army, each regiment being under the command of a Methodist minister. I am indebted to a published communication in a Texas paper some years ago for the leading features in the above reminiscence. I soon decided there would not be much fighting in Texas, for a while at least, so about twenty-five of us who were anxious for a scrap, started on horseback for the Army of Tennessee.

CHAPTER V.

JOIN THE ARMY OF TENNESSEE—WHAT I SAW—
CONCENTRATING AT CORINTH—ASSIGNED TO
DUTY—BATTLE OF SHILOH—SIDNEY JOHNSTON
KILLED—THE RETREAT—WHAT IT COST.

I carried with me a letter of introduction to the
commanding general, Albert Sidney Johnston, from a
life-long friend of his; I also carried an Episcopal
prayer-book, which is now in my possession, and is
cherished as a precious relic, as the fair hand that bestowed it with her blessing has long since been cold
in death. We reached the mouth of Red river in due
time, when we took passage for Memphis, Tenn. The
boat was packed from stem to stern with men on their
way to reinforce the army. On reaching Memphis we
found everything in confusion. Nashville had been
evacuated, and the army was concentrating at
Corinth, Miss., where everything was being shaped up
for a great battle. We joined the cavalcade for
Corinth. The roads were lined with men, wagons,
and artillery, all equipped with the necessary para-
phernalia of war.

When we reached headquarters and I had presented
my letter of introduction to Gen. Johnston, we were
received with that gallant courtesy, so characteristic
of the true soldier. As soon as we were assigned to
duty, we discovered that we had found what we
"long had sought" and had "mourned because we
found it not"—a battle was close at hand.

General Grant had massed a force of forty thousand men at Pittsburg Landing and General Johnston had collected a force of thirty-five thousand to meet him. General Buell was on his way with thirty thousand additional troops, to reinforce Grant.

It was the plan of the Confederate commander to engage Grant, defeat him, then fall upon Buell's flank and crush him.

On Sunday morning, April 6th, both armies were in line of battle near old Shiloh church; and soon the "dance of death" commenced. General Grant's army heroically held their position for some time, but they could not withstand the impetuous onslaught of the Confederates. Just as General Johnston saw that he was carrying everything before him, he fell, mortally wounded and in a few minutes died in the arms of one of his staff officers, Col. Wm. H. Jack.

It was evident, as the day advanced, that Grant's splendid army of forty thousand men was giving away on all parts of the line; and as the sun went down on that bloody field, the whole army was in full retreat. He tried to rally his shattered forces, under cover of his gunboats, which by this time had opened a terriffic fire on our advancing columns, with but very little effect. The heavens were ablaze with bursting shells and the air was thick with sulphurous smoke. We pressed them to the river bank and many lost their lives while trying to cross. Darkness closed the bloody drama.

We were ordered to fall back and camp upon the field, where lay ten thousand brave Confederates dead and dying. We had won the day, and victory

perched upon our banners. We had captured five
thousand prisoners, forty flags, and an immense
amount of army stores.

Our falling back that night was a fatal mistake.
It gave Grant a chance to rally his terribly shattered
and demoralized forces; and it gave Buell time to
come up with reinforcements. The fight was resumed
on the next morning with renewed vigor. Notwithstanding the numerical superiority of the Federals,
aided by their fleet, the Confederates maintained their
position until evening, when Beauregard withdrew in
good order; he was not " driven from the field," as
some writers have falsely stated. He fell back to
Corinth unmolested, having lost all the substantial
fruits of a grand and glorious victory.

I have no desire to detract from the fair renown
of the distinguished general who succeeded to the
Confederate command; there is little doubt, but had
General Johnston's plans been carried out, the whole
Federal army would have fallen into our hands, with
all the territory we had lost regained; fifty thousand
recruits would have been added to our ranks from
Kentucky; our lines would have been established
along the banks of the Ohio, and our own army thundering at the gates of Cincinnati. With the demoral-
izing effect it would have had at the North, and the
successes of our army in Virginia, it is a reasonable
supposition that the war would have closed then and
there. This, I am satisfied, will be the verdict of
posterity when the impartial history of the great
" War Between the States " comes to be written.

Disaster after disaster followed this great military

blunder. Beauregard, finding his position no longer tenable, evacuated Corinth. This enabled the Union army to secure the Memphis and Charleston railroad and hold a line running from Memphis, through Corinth, nearly to Chattanooga. The Confederacy, by this great oversight in not following the advantages gained at Shiloh, received a blow from which she never recovered.

Acts of heroism by commands and individuals were without number. The Eighth Texas regiment, commanded by Major Harrison, went into the fight on the morning of the first day eleven hundred strong, and on the evening of the second day only three hundred responded at "roll-call." This will give some idea of how desperate was the fighting. A cloud of despondency pervaded the entire army.

3 b g

CHAPTER VI.

JOIN MORGAN—RAID INTO TENNESSEE—CAPTURE
OF PULASKI—MADE A PRISONER AT LEBANON—
CAMP CHASE—JOHNSON'S ISLAND—INCIDENTS OF
PRISON LIFE—EXCHANGE—HORRORS OF THE
TRIP BACK TO DIXIE.

It was while at Corinth, shortly after the battle of
Shiloh, that I first met Captain John H. Morgan, who
afterwards became famous as a dashing cavalry officer.
At that time he had command of a small battalion
of cavalry from Kentucky, and was making preparations for a raid into middle Tennessee and southern
Kentucky, which territory was at that time occupied
by the Federals. He was anxious to augment his
force and offered the most flattering inducements for
us to join and accompany him. Anxious to cut ourselves loose from a victorious army on the retreat,
thirty or forty of us formed ourselves into a squad
and joined his command.

Everything being in readiness, on the 12th day of
April, 1862, we drew six days' rations and started
for Tennessee, our little band numbering about three
hundred. They were not cutthroats and desperadoes,
as the enemy at that time chose to designate them,
but in the main were young men of culture and refinement, most of whom had come out from Kentucky
with Morgan and were from the best families of that
State, General Morgan himself being a polished and
chivalrous gentleman.

Nothing occurred worthy of note until we reached the little town of Pulaski, in Tennessee, which we found garrisoned by about four hundred Federal soldiers. A flag of truce was sent in, demanding a surrender, which was refused. Orders were at once passed down the lines to recap guns, which we knew meant "fight." A charge was ordered, and we dashed into the town, where a brisk fight ensued, which lasted but a short time, when they surrendered.

While we were paroling the prisoners a little episode took place, which will bear relating. General Morgan rode a beautiful blooded black mare, with long flowing mane and tail. The ladies of the place being extremely anxious for some souvenir of the victory, fell upon the little animal and trimmed her mane and tail to the hide. The little beauty certainly presented a ludicrous appearance and caused a great deal of merriment at the general's expense.

The Federals soon learned of our operations and sent a large force in pursuit under the Federal General Dupont, who came up with us at Lebanon, Tenn., where a desperate fight took place in the streets of the town, which lasted two hours. Morgan finding himself greatly outnumbered, was forced to withdraw.

A portion of his command had, during the fight, taken refuge in the second story of a brick building used as an "Odd Fellows' hall." This portion of the command, consisting of about twenty-five men, the writer included, were captured. Thus ended our military career for a time at least, and we entered upon a new phase of the war.

We were taken to Nashville under guard and had no reason to complain of our treatment on the way. Lieutenant-colonel Wood, a graduate of West Point and a nephew of the surgeon-general of the United States army, was one of the captured. We were assigned to quarters in the penitentiary building, where we remained for a week. Every day we were visited by ladies from the city, who always brought us some kind of delicacy, which was greatly appreciated by all.

From Nashville we were sent to Camp Chase, Ohio. Camp Chase was by no means a model hotel. It was overcrowded with prisoners, and the accommodations so limited that our stay there was by no means pleasant.

After remaining at Camp Chase for three weeks. mixed up with dirt, filth and vermin, the officers were separated from the privates and sent to Johnson's Island. Johnson's Island is in the bay of Sandusky, where a prison had been located. exclusively for officers. In passing through the country we received many demonstrations of sympathy from the "Copper-heads," as those having Southern proclivities were termed. This element was much stronger in the Western States than many might suppose. We saw no evidence along the route of a terrible war being waged so close at hand; in fact the only pressure they ever felt was in the loss of friends, who had fallen in battle.

When we reached the prison we were subjected to another search, this being the third time we had passed through this ordeal; but they failed each time to find a pair of single-barrel pistols I had concealed in my bootlegs.

We found on our arrival at the Island eleven hundred Confederate officers, who had been captured in different parts of the South. They were a jolly set of fellows.

The quarters were very well arranged, consisting of two-story wooden buildings, located on either side of a broad street, running the whole length of the grounds, the whole enclosed by a high plank fence, with a walk on top, where sentinels could command a view of all that was going on inside. The rooms were arranged with tiers of bunks, one above the other, which would accommodate two persons with a "tight squeeze." Captain Hooper Harris, a warm-hearted, genial gentleman of Nashville, was my bunk-mate.

I would like to dwell upon the peculiar traits of some of my fellow prisoners, for there were men confined within those walls of recognized culture and ability ; but details of men and their actions become tiresome to the reader, especially as there are so many men of genius and note in the country who have suffered similarly. I will make mention, however, of a little circumstance which occurred to one of our number shortly after his capture. He related it to me himself. Colonel Joel E. Battle, of Tennessee, was one of our most distinguished fellow prisoners. He was a true Southern gentleman in every sense of the term. He was captured at Shiloh, and was first taken to St. Louis. While on the boat ascending the river he was anxiously hunted by the curious passengers, who had never seen a "secesh," and were astonished at the handsome and veteranlike appearance of the gallant colonel. Colonel Battle attempted to avoid them, but, finding it impossible, retreated to the pilot-house of the boat. The eager crowd soon discovered and followed him, among whom was a minister of the gospel, who, instead of preaching "Christ, and him crucified," was stimulating volunteers to enlist and fight their Southern brethren. This "wolf in sheep's clothing" walked into the pilot-house, and, with that indelicacy and effrontery which could only emanate from a bad man or a fool, asked Colonel Battle if he had any objection to kneeling with him in prayer. "Of course not," the colonel replied. Then the so-called saint offered a prayer for the United States and for the destruction of all her enemies, *rebels in particular.* When he had finished the colonel thanked him, and asked if he and the others would join him in prayer, to which they readily agreed. It was something, I am confident, that Colonel Battle had never undertaken before in public. At it the colonel went, praying with a will for the Southern Confederacy, and the destruction of all her enemies, Yankees in particular. Rising from his knees, he exclaimed, with an air, as those only who knew Colonel Battle as we did, can appreciate: "Now, I'll bet you, or any other man, a hundred dollars that my prayer reached heaven first." The colonel assured us that he was not troubled by vulgar curiosity during the rest of the trip.

One of the most courtly gentlemen in prison was

Lieutenant Legendre. He was a young creole of
New Orleans, and a cousin of General Beauregard's.
His companion, Lieutenant D'Aubigne, from the same
city, was a descendent of the writer of that name.
These young Frenchmen were disinterested patriots,
having left affluence and position behind them to
face disease, death and imprisonment for the cause
they had espoused. They felt that it was no disgrace
to be a prisoner. LaFayette languished in prison,
and so had some of the great and good of all ages.
Colonel Olmstead, of the First Volunteer Regiment
of Georgia, was confined with us on the bleak shores
of that far-away inland sea. He was a gentleman in
or out of prison. His gallant defense of Fort Pulaski is a matter of history.

Few circles were ever adorned with a brighter social element than, by the fortunes of war, were thrown
together on Johnson's Island in the summer of 1862.
Eleven hundred men, representing different States,
and of peculiar characteristics, thrown together in a
mass, furnished a fine field for moral and intellectual
dissection.

The monotony of prison life was relieved in various ways. A number of games were instituted.
Quite a mechanical genius was developed by many
in carving rings from bone, shirt buttons, breastpins
and numerous other trinkets from beautiful shells
which we picked up on the beach of the lake while
bathing. (We were allowed to take a bath in the
lake every evening.)

Our rations were the same as issued to the soldiers
in the army, and were all of a substantial character.

The sick were well cared for by the surgeon in charge. The Sabbath was well observed. Every Sunday service was held by some one of the many ministers confined in the prison. Several deaths occurred during our stay on the island. A funeral at sea is a melancholy spectacle. The gloomy looks of the crew, the dejected expression of weeping relatives, seem to fill the imagination with all that is distressing and heartrending. Yet the freshness of the ocean breeze, new and changing scenes, the excitement of storm, with the whirl of life 'midst the hundreds on shipboard, softens, if not effaces, the shadows of death at sea, but 'tis not so in prison. The soldier dies, and his body is placed in a common pine coffin, a little wagon is sent in, and the coffin is placed in it; the driver cracks his whip, and the vehicle rattles away over the ruts and clods of the campus to a little spot outside, where he is laid to rest beside his comrades with no living hand to place a garland on his lonely grave. It is to be hoped that steps will be taken to remove the remains of those who died at Johnson's Island, and deposit their bones somewhere in the South, the land they loved so well and for which they gave their lives.

Many ladies visited the prison during the summer, and it was through the kindness of our post-surgeon, Dr. Woodbridge, to whom their admittance was due. Most of them were from the South, and had trveled long distances to communicate with friends and relatives. Quite a patriotic incident occurred in this connection, of which I will make brief mention, showing a mother's undying devotion to the honor of her child.

A young lieutenant, a native of Boston, Mass., but who had resided in the South prior to the war, and had cast his fortunes with the Southern Confederacy, was captured in one of the engagements and sent to Johnson's Island. Shortly after reaching prison, he was taken with a fever which he had contracted while soldiering in the swamps of the Mississippi. He requested that his mother, who still lived in Boston, be written to. His request was complied with, and his mother arrived in a few days. She was at once conducted to his bedside. Her general deportment indicated a lady of intelligence, wealth and refinement. Under her gentle and affectionate nursing her son was soon convalescent. She was quite anxious for him to return home with her. There was but one way, however, by which this desire could be gratified, and that was to take the oath of allegiance to the United States Government. When she ascertained that fact, her eyes moistened and she said: "However much I would like to have my son with me, where he could live in comfort and ease, far away from the pains of this cruel war, I had rather see him brought home a corpse than come home *dishonored.*" No Spartan mother ever evinced a nobler spirit. The young gentleman had considered the matter well before taking the step which made him a Confederate soldier and an alien from the United States. He soon recovered and when exchanged, rejoined his command and was twice promoted for gallantry on the field.

I met him just after the war closed at Memphis, Tenn., on his way to pay his mother a visit. He had been wounded twice, which caused a slight limp. He afterwards became a prosperous merchant in one of our Southern cities.

Hundreds of Northern young men, who were living in the South when the war broke out, joined the Southern army, and made brave and gallant soldiers. Many of them occupied distinguished positions, and were regarded by all as loyal to the cause they had espoused.

Our custodians at Johnson's Island would, at times, try their hand at arbitrary measures, and how well they succeeded in carrying them out the following incident will show: An order had been published that all prisoners should retire to their quarters at retreat (sundown), the only period of the day when it was possible to be comfortable. Lieutenant Gibson had been spending the afternoon with a comrade, about twenty steps from his quarters. On hearing the signal, he hastily returned to his room, and had one foot on the threshold when the sentinel, without any warning, shot him down in cold blood. The entire charge entered his body, and he died in a few moments. It was a dastardly act. What was ever done, if anything, with the perpetrator of this diabolical outrage we never learned. It is a cowardly act to maltreat a prisoner, and I never knew an old soldier to be guilty of it.

On the first day of September, 1862, we took our departure from Johnson's Island. A cartel had been agreed upon for an exchange of prisoners. We were again to taste the fresh air of freedom; to bid farewell to Johnson's Island, where we had been confined for four months as prisoners of war. There was great rejoicing when the announcement was made, and we left the place with very little regret, as was evidenced by the following lines, copied from the wall of one of our prison buildings, penciled by an unknown hand:

" Hoarse sounding billows of the white-capped lake,
That 'gainst the barriers of our hated prison break,
Farewell! farewell! thou giant inland sea;
Thou, too, subservest the modes of tyranny—
Girding this isle, washing its lonely shore
With moaning echoes of thy melancholy roar;
Farewell, thou lake! Farewell, thou inhospitable land!
Thou hast the curses of this patriot band —
All, save the spot, the holy sacred bed,
Where rest in peace our Southern warriors, dead."

We were not long in making the necessary preparations for a start. Our baggage was not at all burdensome; what few effects we had we wrapped in an old army blanket and swung it about our necks. We were transported by boat to Sandusky; then huddled into box-cars like so many cattle, and started on our run for the South, Cairo, Ill., being our objective point. We were on the cars thirty-six hours in that packed condition. Our suffering was extreme.

I had learned enough while in prison and during our transfer to the Southern border, to know that the subjugation of the South was but a question of time. The armies of the North were splendidly equipped, with any amount of the finest guns and munitions of war from the workshops of Europe, while the Confederates, cut off from the world, had to rely solely upon the hastily constructed factories they had set up, and the guns and stores they captured from the enemy. The Federal Government had every facility for drawing from the surplus population of Europe in countless numbers to fill up the shattered ranks of their armies. The people of our homes were kept in a fever of excitement by the newspaper accounts of the operations at the front. The Northern papers would exaggerate their successes and conceal their defeats.

At Cairo, at that time a city of filth and bad smells, we were stowed away on board an old tug, sometimes called a steamboat (by those who had an elastic veracity), with but one small stove on which eleven hundred men were to cook their meals. We were conveyed down the river by two Federal gunboats, one in front and one in the rear. We only traveled in the day-time, which made our sufferings much more severe, as we were eleven days on the river from Cairo to Vicksburg, when the trip should have been made in five days. Our treatment by some of the subordinates was frightfully cruel; for this, however, we could not hold the government responsible. We would frequently receive encouraging demonstrations from the shores as we passed along.

CHAPTER VII.

LAND IN VICKSBURG—OUR FORLORN CONDITION—
MY FAITHFUL SERVANT MEETS AND CONSOLES
ME—GO TO JACKSON—MORGAN GONE TO KEN-
TUCKY—EFFORTS TO JOIN HIM—FORM PART OF
AN INTERESTING AND PLEASANT PARTY—COL.
HUNDLEY'S DIARY—BRAGG'S RETREAT—BUSH-
WHACKERS—MIDNIGHT FIGHT—BREAKING UP
AN OUTLAW BAND—BACK TO KNOXVILLE—
MEET MORGAN AT BLACK'S SHOP.

On the seventeenth day of September, 1862, ever
memorable to the Confederate soldiers who formed
that human cargo from Johnson's Island, we stepped
on shore in Dixie. How different from a few
months before! No demonstration of friendly feeling; not a flag unfurled; not even a handkerchief
waved! The rain was pouring down in torrents as
we passed out into the muddy streets of the "Hill
City."

We were a pitiable sight, drenched to the skin.
The first friendly face to greet the writer as I stepped
from the boat was that of my negro boy, Bob, who
was captured with me and taken as far as Camp
Chase, Ohio, where he, with the rest of the servants,
was turned loose among strangers. This was their
first taste of freedom, but they had no relish for it,
and all worked their way back to the command.
When Bob found that I was to be exchanged, he
got permission from the commanding officer to go
to Vicksburg to meet me. The poor fellow clapped

his hands and jumped with joy when he first saw me.
Great big tears would well up in his eyes, and I
thought, for a time, he would go crazy.

Six thousand of us were adrift in Vicksburg,
without shelter, clothes or food—a gloomy time.
While slopping along the streets hunting for shelter
I met my old room-mate at Johnson's Island, Captain Harris, on the same mission. He greeted me
with the remark, "I had rather die in Vicksburg
than any other place I was ever in.".

"Why so, Captain?" I asked.

"Because I could leave it with less regret," he
replied.

The captain, myself and Bob found shelter under
an awning, where we spread our wet blankets and
piled down together and enjoyed a comfortable (?)
nights' sleep.

The next day we were sent on to Jackson, where
we found General Tilgham, one of the most distinguished officers in the Confederate army. He had
been delegated to receive the exchanged prisoners
and pay them off. Every facility was extended to
us in Jackson for our comfort. We remained there
but a few days, all being anxious to get back to our
respective commands, who were making history.

General Morgan, with his command, had gone
with Bragg into Kentucky. He left us a message to
go on to Knoxville, Tenn., and from there to cross
the mountains at Cumberland Gap and join him.
We remained in Jackson a few days to recruit; then,
with haversacks well filled with the substantials of
life, provided by the kind ladies of the place (to

whom we have ever felt grateful), we bade adieu to the capital city of Mississippi.

At every station along the route we were greeted with patriotic tokens of encouragement. This was strikingly conspicuous, when contrasted with the demonstrations we witnessed while passing through the cold and inhospitable North.

At Knoxville we drew the necessary supplies for our trip. The quartermaster turned over to us some government horses, so we were not long in getting fairly equipped.

I met General John C. Breckenridge at Knoxville, who, with a portion of his division, was on his way to join Bragg in Kentucky. At that time I thought he was the finest looking man I had ever seen in the saddle, and I believe that was the universal verdict. He looked older than when I saw him last, at Corinth, some months previous.

The boys were very much elated at the prospect of once more treading the soil of their native State, and assisting in hurling back the invaders from the land they loved so well. But they were doomed to disappointment.

We met a number of officers who had been absent on detailed service, and were collecting a party to cross the mountains and join their commands; among whom was Colonel Hundley, a very pleasant and affable gentleman, of Alabama. He expressed great gratification on learning that our party was on the same mission and requested that we act as their escort, which was readily acceded to, for the section through which we were to pass was considered quite

dangerous, the mountains being infested with " bushwhackers."

After the lapse of thirty years, no man can rely on
his memory as well as the record of events, written
at the time of their occurrence.   I kept no diary and
will encroach upon a portion of a diary kept by Colonel Hundley, which was afterwards written up by
him for the Philadelphia *Evening Journal.*   Colonel
H. says, in regard to our trip from Knoxville to
Kentucky: " Our escort declared ready to serve us,
" and we left Knoxville at 1 P. M., October 11th,
" 1862.   We only traveled ten miles to-day.   Our
" escort consists of thirty-five men, exchanged pris-
" oners, just from Camp Chase and Johnson's Island.
" They formerly belonged to Colonel John H. Mor-
" gan's original band, now so famous.   They, with
" Captain Austin, who commands the squad, were
" captured at Lebanon, Tenn.   I am certainly not
" afraid to take chances with such a noble-looking
" set of fellows, among the Union jayhawkers and
" bushwhackers, now infesting mountain fastnesses,
" all the way from Cumberland Gap to the open re-
" gion of Kentucky.   Besides our escort there are
" several officers in our company.   Major Nocquet,
" Bragg's Chief of Engineers, a little, polite, black-
" bearded Frenchman, has with him his ambulance,
" which carries most of the provisions for myself and
" brother officers.   The escort has two wagons to
" carry our forage, etc.   Major Wickliffe, a tall, free-
" and-easy Kentuckian, and son of the Union Con-
" gressman of that name, with Adjutant Purtle, are
" accompanying us on a visit to their homes, in ad-

" vance of Breckenridge's command, to which they
" belong. The command is expected to leave Knox-
" ville soon. Captain Steel, of the engineers, accom-
" panies Major Nocquet. My old friend, Captain
" Henderson, is also with us, on his way to rejoin his
" regiment. Altogether, we are a very pleasant com-
" pany, and around our camp-fire to-night have had
" some lively discussions about the situation of affairs,
" both in Tennessee and Kentucky, as well as in other
" portions of the South.

" We traveled about thirty miles to-day (October
" 12th), in spite of the rain. We succeeded in cross-
" ing the Clinch river soon after dark. The more I
" see of my traveling companions, the better I am
" pleased with them. They are certainly a lively
" crowd, full of anecdotes of stirring adventure by
" flood and field. Around our camp-fire to-night we
" had an animated discussion as to the future of our
" new republic. Major Nocquet maintained, with his
" foreign shrug, that, so far, Democracy had proved
" to be a failure, and that nothing but a monarchy
" can ever heal our dissensions. I grieve to say that
" some of my brother officers were inclined to agree
" with him, but the discussion served to arouse me
" from gloomy reflections, and I combated their ideas
" to the best of my ability. I am for a republic, to-
" day, to-morrow, and for all time.

" We crossed the Cumberland Gap just before dark
" and are now in camp at the foot of the mountain on
" its Kentucky side.

" We have just learned that there has been some
" hard fighting in Kentucky. Nevertheless we col-

4 b к

"lect about our blazing fire and fight over again our
"famous battles, while Major Nocquet favors us oc-
"casionally with a snatch of that marvelous song—

"'*Allons enfants de la partrie, le jour de gloire est
arrivé.*'

BRAGG IN RETREAT.

"We are stopping to-night, the 14th, about five
"miles from Barboursville, in one of the most noto-
"rious Union settlements in Kentucky.

"Our ride to-day was through a country rugged,
"picturesque and beautiful. The overhanging cliffs
"are even grand at times.

"We have had bad news. It is said that Bragg's
"army is retreating from Kentucky. We can hardly
"credit this report, but fear it is only too true. The
"Kentuckians with us are exceedingly sorrowful and
"refuse to be comforted. Major Wickliffe is swear-
"ing more than our army did in Flanders.

"We made no move to-day, the 15th, except to
"take up our quarters in a country church and await
"events. It is evident that we need go no further.
"There can be no longer any doubt about Bragg's army
"being on the retreat. The advance of his wagon-train
"reached here this morning, and has been passing by us
"all day. They are loaded down with stores, captured
"by our forces while in Kentucky. We learn from
"the officers in charge that there was a bloody fight
"at Perryville, in which we were the victors. They
"expressed themselves as unable to account for
"the order to retreat. As the day advanced, the evi-
"dences of a grand 'skeedaddle' became more and

" more conspicuous. Besides the wagons there has
" been passing immense trains of mules, great herds
" of fat cattle, and regiments of stragglers, together
" with thousands of fleeing citizens, male and female.
" Some of them are in carriages, and have along nu-
" merous contrabands. They are in a hurry to get
" out of the way as fast as possible. The great army
" of wagons, mules, horses, stragglers and fleeing cit-
" izens has continued all day to pass by us like a great
" caravan. The spectacle certainly surpassed any-
" thing I had ever before witnessed. John Morgan's
" men have already proven to be his true followers.

" While his men were entertaining themselves
" about camp, Captain Austin, a tall, stout, square-
" built Texan about twenty-five years of age, was also
" busy. He had found out, by some means, that for
" some time an old Union man in the neighborhood
" had made his house a sort of headquarters for a
" band of mounted guerillas. His house was ordered
" to be searched. When, lo ! it was discovered to be
" a perfect arsenal. We drew from its hidden reces-
" ses nearly a hundred splendid United States sabers,
" with rifles, muskets, cartridges, etc, until our coun-
" try church looked like an arsenal indeed, bristling
" with so many weapons of war.

" There was another noteworthy incident of the
" day. We arrested an old Unionist, taking him to
" our church under guard. We kept him in durance
" vile until nearly dark, hoping to make him tell us
" where the band of jayhawkers lay concealed. He
" persistently refused to tell anything, and Captain
" Austin suggested that we dispose of him summarily

"as a spy. This was done, after consultation with
"myself and others, simply to frighten him. The old
"fellow seemed greatly concerned for awhile, and
"begged to be permitted to send for his wife and lit-
"tle children. They soon put in an appearance. It
"was a pitiful sight. I could withstand his wife's
"entreaties, with dry eyes, knowing, as I did, that
"we designed bringing her husband to no harm, but
"when one of his little boys crept up to his side, the
"big tears rolling down his cheeks, and took from
"his pocket a couple of large, red apples, which he
"tremblingly handed to his parent, saying, artlessly :
"'Father, I thought you might be hungry,' I could
"resist no longer. I wiped the mist from my eyes
"and bade the old gentleman go home.

"Captain Austin and his men left early this
"morning, taking along the captured arms."

This ends the account of our trip from Knoxville
to the border of Kentucky, as noted by Colonel Hundley at the time.

While at the old church, we received notice from
General Morgan to return to Knoxville and there remain until we heard from him. He was making his
way out of Kentucky toward the West, and would
halt his command at some point in Middle Tennessee.

By the time we were ready to take the back-track
our little band had been largely reinforced by young
men who had come out from Kentucky to join the
army. They were well mounted and thoroughly
equipped for service.

We parted from the officers who had accompanied

us, with many regrets. They were a splendid set of fellows.

I became convinced, by the large amount of arms we had captured, that there was a regularly organized band of bushwhackers in that vicinity; and as we were anxious for a little active service on our own hook, I decided to make an effort to locate them. In order to do so it became necessary that we move with very great caution. With that object in view, we quietly recrossed the mountain and went into camp about three miles west of the path we had traveled a few days before. I did this because our supplies were running short, and the stragglers and bummers from Bragg's army had about cleaned up the country. What they could not buy with Confederate money they took with unblushing impudence. Chickens, turkeys, ducks, geese, pigs, sheep; in fact everything that could walk or fly was shot down and carried off on their shoulders, kicking and squealing. It was a most humiliating spectacle. What must have been the opinion of the Union citizens of Kentucky of such soldiers? We certainly gained few friends by such dastardly conduct.

Bragg's army suffered from hunger, thirst, exposure and forced marches on his retreat from Kentucky, but most of all, from hunger and thirst. For several days they subsisted on parched corn, and drank water from filthy pools, in which lay the carcasses of dead mules. It was a sad sight to see the veterans of Bragg's army passing. For hours I looked on with melancholy emotions. Regiment after regiment passed, waving their blood-stained ban-

ners, many of them torn and riddled with balls of
many a hotly contested fight.

We located our camp in a pleasant valley where
we could procure forage for our horses. I selected
five men and a trusty guide from my old command to
reconnoitre the country for the headquarters of the
outlaws, and in order to avoid any suspicion or at-
tract attention to our movements, postponed our departure until after dark. Our guide informed us that
about ten miles distant, at the head of a valley, there
lived a family who were in strong sympathy with the
Southern movement; there we were likely to gain
information. We reached the house without seeing
or hearing anything to our advantage. Halting six
or eight hundred yards away, in a clump of undergrowth, Captain Roberts, the guide and myself dismounted, leaving our horses in charge of the other
men, with instructions if they heard firing to come
to us at once. On reaching the house we discovered
a dim light through the window. We satisfied ourselves that there was no person outside, then proceeded,
with few gentle raps, to arouse the inmates. After
some little time a lady cautiously approached the
window, raised it a trifle, and in a suppressed voice
asked what was wanted. I replied that we had
learned that she was a lady of strong Southern proclivities, and that we were seeking information in
regard to a band of jayhawkers located somewhere
in that vicinity. After we convinced her that we
were Southern soldiers she opened the door, and Captain Roberts and myself went in, the guide remaining outside to watch.

" Yes," she said, after bidding us be seated; "my whole feeling is with the Southern cause. My husband and one son are now with Lee, in Virginia. Myself, a sister and a small negro boy are the only occupants of this house."

" Where is the negro boy at this time?" I asked.

" He is fast asleep in a back-room."

" Is there not a possibility of his overhearing our conversation?" I then asked.

" Not in the least. I think, gentlemen, that I may be able to give you all the information about these robbers you may desire. Oh, they have treated us outrageously! Unfortunately, they have stolen nearly everything we have. We live right in the midst of them."

She was a lady of intelligence and spoke with much animation.

" These men have for a long time been a terror to this whole community, robbing indiscriminately, Union as well as Confederate families, until we have little left. I do so much wish they could be broken up, and will render you all the assistance I can. But we must be very cautious. It would never do for them to find out that I had given any information, for they would burn us out and murder us. Only night-before-last five of them came riding up to my house and ordered me to cook supper for them. While busy preparing their meal I overheard them discussing some of their plans. Their rendezvous is about three miles from here, in an old log school-house, which I understand they have strongly fortified. There are about forty or fifty in the gang when

they are all together. Their captain is the noted
desperado, Gus Summers. He is a strong, powerful
man, about thirty-five years old. He was considered
a bad man before the war commenced, and every one
was afraid of him. He came into this settlement
about two years before the war, and every one thought
he was an escaped convict from somewhere. From
what I could learn from the five men that were at
my house they are to hold an important meeting at
the old schoolhouse on next Saturday night. I have
no doubt but that the most of them will be there."

Upon this information I at once decided to exam-
ine the place and find out what I could about the
location. It was then Friday night, and we had
but scant time to procure the necessary information,
get back to camp and be on hand the next night
ready for any emergency.

After getting directions how to reach the place we
bade the kind lady good-bye, with a strict injunction
to say nothing to any one, not even her sister, about
our being there, until she heard from us again. We
returned to our horses, found everything all right,
and were soon on our way to the headquarters of the
guerillas. Our directions were so comprehensive that
we had no difficulty in finding the spot. We found
that the old schoolhouse had been converted into
quite a formidable fortress. There were two doors
standing opposite each other, which were strongly
barricaded. The house stood just at the foot of the
mountain, and a rock breastwork had been placed in
front. I fixed well in my mind all the approaches;
then we started for our horses, which were a mile

away. We were soon in the saddle and on our way back to camp, which we reached just as day was breaking.

After a rest of a few hours I went about making preparations for our night's work. We were forced to be very quiet about it, in order to prevent any suspicion being aroused in the minds of outsiders. I selected forty determined men, not one of them knowing the object of the move, except the five who were with me the night before. They were given to understand, however, that we were going on a perilous expedition, and must have everything in readiness by dark. The night proved favorable for our operations, as a slight rain commenced falling about dusk and continued most of the night.

Leaving the camp in charge of Lieutenant Stikes, a little after dark we quietly withdrew. Every man had been instructed that there must be no talking—simply to hold themselves in readiness for any emergency. At eleven o'clock we reached a spot within a mile of the old schoolhouse, where we had agreed to call a halt. Captain Roberts and myself then went on foot to survey the grounds and make what discoveries we could.

The rain was still falling; the night was dark and chilly. As we approached the house we could see a faint light glimmering through the cracks, and could distinctly hear voices within. A smoldering fire was burning in the old fire-place, the only light visible. As near as we could judge there were twenty-five or thirty men inside, and from what we could glean from their conversation they were planning an attack on some wagon train. They evidently had no apprehension of being molested that night, as they had placed no guard outside. When we satisfied ourselves with the outlook we returned to our men, and informed them of the nature of our expedition and what would be expected of them.

I dismounted thirty men, and left ten with the horses, as the work in hand was to be accomplished on foot. I stationed one man on horse-back, within two or three hundred yards of the house, with orders, the moment he heard firing, to return immediately and bring up the horses. A short distance from the house we secured two pieces of timber, which had been used as a foot-way across a creek; these we utilized as battering-rams. I directed Captain Roberts, with ten men and one of the sticks of timber, to take his position at the back door while I took mine at the front.

All being in readiness, at a given signal, both doors went down with a crash, and our men jumped through the openings. Then the "dance of death" commenced.

The place, which but a few moments before was as still as the grave was now the scene of a desperate conflict. In less time than it takes to tell it, twelve of the outlaws were stretched dead on the floor and as many more desperately wounded. They fought like demons! Captain Roberts, upon entering the door, stumbled and fell. A big, burly mountaineer jumped forward and was in the act of dealing him a deadly blow with a saber, when a well-directed shot from my pistol brought him down. Roberts was soon on his feet and doing splendid execution. The leader of the gang was stretched at full length in the middle of the room, with a dozen bullet holes through his body. After their leader fell, all that were not killed or wounded threw up their hands and cried for quarter, and were at once made prisoners.

I believe it was one of the bloodiest hand-to-hand encounters that took place during the war, and resulted in more benefit to the people of that section than Bragg's fruitless march into Kentucky. We had broken up a band of lawless desperadoes, composed of deserters from both armies. Even women and children were victims of their atrocious crimes. We had one man killed and five wounded in the scrap. The wounds were soon dressed by our surgeon and the men made as comfortable as circumstances would permit.

With our horses picketed outside, we waited for daylight that we might view the dreadful carnage. The old schoolhouse had gone through a regular baptism of blood. The morning was bright and pleasant. A detail was sent out to procure forage and five men dispatched to Lieutenant Stikes to bring up our wagon-train.

The dead outlaws were buried with but very little ceremony by the citizens of the neighborhood.

We captured forty or fifty six-shooters, as many rifles and sabers, with a big lot of ammunition. We secured a quantity of provisions which was stowed away under the house, evidently for the purpose of withstanding a siege. Twenty-five fine Kentucky horses also fell into our hands. The wounded desperadoes were sent to the houses near by to be cared for, while our wounded soldiers were carried with us.

By ten o'clock the scene of our night's exploit was thronged with people, mostly old men, women and children from the surrounding country. The news of the fight had spread like wild-fire. All classes were loud in their congratulations at our success in effectually breaking up this notorious band of marauders who had so long been a terror to the people.

I remunerated the kind lady who furnished us the information, by turning over to her a good horse, some provisions and a snug little purse of greenbacks —Confederate money being of very little use in that part of the country.

Our wagon-train having reported, we made hasty preparations and pushed on to Knoxville.

The news of our little adventure with the bush-whackers had reached the town in advance of us and, as usual, was considerably magnified. We received congratulations on every hand for our brilliant achievement, as the newspapers thought proper to designate it.

CHAPTER VIII.

BACK AT KNOXVILLE—COL. ST. LEDGER GRANFEL—
MORALE OF BRAGG'S ARMY—BOTH ARMIES PRE-
PARING FOR BATTLE—9TH KENTUCKY CAVALRY
ORGANIZED—MORGAN'S MARRIAGE—THOSE PANTS
—INTO KENTUCKY—CAPTURE AT BARDSTOWN—
AT MULDROUGH'S HILL—AT CYNTHIANA—THAT
TELEGRAPH OPERATOR.

I met, for the first time, while in Knoxville, Colonel St. Ledger Granfel, an eccentric Englishman,
who claimed that he had been in the English service
over thirty years and had come over to teach us how
to fight. He rendered himself quite conspicuous by
relating his many adventures and hair-breadth escapes
in different parts of the world. He acted for awhile
as Morgan's Inspector-General, but his English ways
didn't suit our boys, who became very much dissatis-
fied with him—in fact so much so that General Morgan was compelled to remove him. With sword in
hand, he took his leave, saying that he would return
to old "Hingland," and report to her Royal Majesty.
We all hoped he would meet with more congenial
spirits than he had found among Morgan's raiders.

Bragg's march into Kentucky was disastrous in
many respects. Widespread demoralization pervaded the whole army. He was censured on every hand.
The troops had lost confidence in him. The road
from Knoxville to Chattanooga was lined with stragglers and there were hundreds of desertions.

We remained in camp near Knoxville two weeks;

(61)

then learned that Morgan had crossed the mountains, back into Tennessee and was somewhere in the vicinity of Murfreesboro. We made haste to join him, for we were exceedingly anxious to once more get back to our old command, after an absence of many months.

On reaching Morgan's camp at a little place called "Black's Shop," we found that he had largely augmented his forces by his recent campaign into Kentucky. His army at that time numbered about three thousand men. They had much to discourage them, but their hopes were somewhat stimulated by a prospect of again entering Kentucky. Morgan lost no time in reorganizing his men preparatory to a contemplated raid in the rear of the Federal army, which was concentrating near Nashville, under General Rosecrans. Bragg was massing his army at Murfreesboro. Although his troops were greatly dispirited, they were ready and willing to meet the enemy when and wherever directed. Morgan had been ordered to go to the rear of Rosecrans's army and harass his communications. With a view to that end, he at once went about getting things in shape. He organized a new regiment, composed of separate detachments that had been added to his command, and numbered it the "Ninth Kentucky."

By this time Morgan's name and fame had become so well established as a dashing cavalry leader, that recruits were coming to him every day. William C. P. Breckenridge was made Colonel; R. J. Stoner, Lieutenant-Colonel; and the writer, Major of the new regiment. It was a splendid body of men; most of them from the very best families of Kentucky. Many

of them had, but a short time previous, left the class-
room in college, to cast their fortunes with the Confederacy. J. J. C. Black, at this time a member of
Congress from Georgia, was one of that number.
He was an accomplished orator, a high-toned,
chivalrous gentleman, and one who could always be
relied upon implicitly, under any and all circumstances. Colonel Breckenridge, a descendant of
one of the oldest and most distinguished families of the South, was a gentleman of marked
ability, and inherited many of the noble quali-
ties and lofty attributes of his illustrous ancestors. For many years he represented the Ashland
district in Congress, and was universally acknowledged as the silver-tongued orator of the South.
Lieutenant-Colonel Stoner was a descendant of one of
the oldest and wealthiest families in Kentucky. He
had an eye like an eagle and knew no such word as
fear. He was a pleasant, genial gentleman, but
when aroused, was a host within himself. No braver
soldier ever drew his sword in defense of the South,
than Colonel Bob Stoner. Dr. A. T. Pearsall, who
was made surgeon of the regiment, was in Europe,
completing his medical studies, when the war commenced; and while the guns of Beauregard were
thundering away at the walls of Sumter, he was on
his way across the Atlantic, to offer his services to
the "Bleeding South," the land of his nativity. Education and intercourse with the best society had
stamped him a gentleman. Though quite young, he
was master of his profession. His quiet deportment,

gentle and impressive urbanity, went far to ameliorate the sufferings of many a wounded soldier.

An event took place at this time which I do not feel justified in passing over. General Morgan had, for some time, as occasion would permit, been paying his addresses to one of Tennessee's fairest daughters. She was Miss Reedy, the daughter of Judge Reedy, of Murfreesboro. Miss Reedy, a few days previous to the occurrence I am about to narrate, had passed through the Federal lines and was stopping at the house of a friend, not far distant from the location of our command. The day before we were to start on our raid, it was rumored about camp that the General was to be married to the beautiful and accomplished young Tennesseean.

I met General Morgan in the evening, as he was returning from a little scout on his own hook. During the conversation, I asked him if there was any foundation for the rumor that was floating about camp as to the happy event. With one of his pleasant smiles and a peculiar twinkle of the eye, he said : " They have got it down about right, and it will take place just after the command leaves in the morning." He added that he was somewhat perplexed as to a suitable pair of pants for the occasion. " General, I remarked, I think I can assist you in your dilemma. A few days ago we captured an ambulance, and in it was some baggage which, I judged, belonged to some Federal officer. In looking it over, I came across a pair of blue broadcloth pants, with a gold cord down the seam. I took no particular notice of them at the time, but I am under the impression that they will till the bill." "All right," he replied, "Send them to my quarters to-night, and if they will fit, they will be just what I have been looking for." Exchanging salutes we parted. The pants proved to be a perfect fit. The wedding was a quiet affair, only a few friends being present. After the ceremony, cake and wine were served; then the gay cavaliers mounted their horses, waved the bride "adieu," and were off to overtake the command, which they accomplished after a few hours' hard riding. The first obstruction we met with was at Bardstown, Kentucky, where, after a hard fight of over an hour we captured the garrison of over a thousand men, who were paroled, as it would draw too heavily from our command to furnish an adequate guard to conduct them safely to the rear. A large amount of supplies fell into our hands; what we could not use we destroyed.

Then we hastened to the Louisville and Nashville Railroad at Muldrough's Hill, where there was an immense trestle, spanning a stream of water which we found guarded by four hundred and eighty of the seventy-first Indiana regiment. After a brisk fight, which lasted but a short time they surrendered.

We destroyed the trestle, cut all the telegraph wires, then waited for a train which was expected to arrive from Louisville in an hour. The train soon came thundering around the curve and it was flagged down. It was heavily loaded with army supplies. On board were about fifty Federal officers, who were on their way to join their commands at Nashville, a number of them having their wives with them. The

ladies were, naturally, excited when they learned
that they were in the hands of Morgan's raiders, as
they had heard so many exaggerated accounts of them,
but, as was our custom, they were treated with the
utmost consideration and were soon pacified upon being
assured that no harm would come to them. Their
baggage without being molested was placed in
country wagons and sent back to Louisville, and the
officers were paroled, to report inside of our lines
within ten days. General Morgan demanded on all
such occasions that proper courtesy should be shown
to ladies. After taking from the train such supplies
as we needed, we set fire to it and sent it crashing
over the embankment, where we had burned the
trestle. It was a grand sight to see that blazing
train go down to destruction! We captured a large
United States mail, which furnished the boys reading
matter for a week. Just as we had completed our
work of destruction at that point we learned that a
large Federal force had been sent in pursuit of us;
but, as Morgan never let the grass grow under his
feet, we were soon off, with little apprehension of the
Yanks overtaking us. We always kept our tracks
well covered, by keeping all lines of communication
cut off.

We struck the town of Cynthiana about daylight,
and captured a small Federal garrison without firing
a gun. As was his custom, Morgan at once repaired
to the telegraph office where he found the operator
quietly sleeping on a lounge. When Morgan aroused
him from his slumbers, and asked the news, he, in a
very boastful and indignant spirit, stated that they

had heard, the evening before, that Morgan was in the State and "playing the wild" with 'the railroads. He remarked, by way of prelude, that he would regard it the greatest achievement of his life if he could only put an end to the notorious outlaw.

Morgan, with one of his bland smiles, asked: "And would you really slay the rebel chieftain, if you had the opportunity?"

"Yes," he replied, "then I would be willing to die myself, after conferring such an inestimable blessing on the country."

"Well, then," said the general, "if those are truly your sentiments, have thy wish." He then drew a pair of glittering revolvers from his belt, and, handing one to the operator, said: "Now, young man, crown yourself with glory. This is John Morgan."

The fellow wilted, turned pale as a sheet, and commenced mumbling out some kind of an apology. Morgan said to him:

"I have this to say to you: take your seat at that instrument and send forward to Louisville such a dispatch as I shall dictate. If you make a single bobble it will cost you your life."

It is hardly necessary to say that he complied to the letter.

Morgan sent several dispatches in regard to the movement of troops, as coming from a Federal officer. He also sent one to George D. Prentiss, at that time editor of the Louisville Journal, asking him if he knew anything about the whereabouts of Morgan, lately.

" No," he replied; "at the same time, I would not
be surprised to wake up and find him in bed with me
any morning."

We had secured a large amount of army stores;
destroyed bridges, railroads and telegraph lines; captured and paroled over four thousand prisoners,
many more than the entire number of men we took
into Kentucky; besides receiving many recruits; and
we lost only twenty or twenty-five men in all the
bloody conflicts in which we were engaged. They
were of but little avail, however, as they could not
be followed up, as the enemy had such extensive
resources to draw from. By this means they were
soon able to repair the damages.

CHAPTER IX.

AT McMINNVILLE—ON BRAGG'S FLANKS—MORGAN'S
PLAN FOR CARRYING ON THE WAR—MORGAN AS
A SPY—CAPTURE ON THE LEBANON PIKE—"THE
PATHFINDER "— HIS HEARTRENDING STORY —
ORDERED TO BRAGG'S HEADQUARTERS—GO TO
CHATTANOOGA — MY FRIEND THE FEDERAL
OFFICER A WOUNDED PRISONER—I MINISTER TO
HIM—HIS EXCHANGE.

On our return General Morgan established his
headquarters at McMinnville, Tenn., and had distributed his forces on the right flank of Bragg's
army, for scouting and picket service.

During our absence in Kentucky the battle of
Stone River had been fought between the armies of
Bragg and Rosecrans. Without entering into details, I will say that it was one of the bloodiest
battles of the war. The Federals called it a drawn
battle, but from all the facts that could be obtained
at the time, it was regarded as a victory for the Confederates.

Bragg, as usual, fell back and failed to gain any
advantage from the result; in fact, he lost by it. His
army was weakened, and the soldiers had become
despondent. They could see but little hope of
ever establishing the independence of the South.
Even at that time, when all looked dark and gloomy,
and the Federal lines, anaconda-like, were gradually
tightening their coils around the doomed Confederacy, if a change of policy had been adopted, we

would have gained all we had lost. We had stood
on the defense long enough.

Morgan's plan was to mount Bragg's entire army,
form them in two columns, under competent leaders,
invade the North by moving in parallel lines; while
a third column was formed in Virginia to operate in
conjunction. Let all push, by rapid marches, into
the Northern States, destroying all public property
and lines of communication. The Federals would
not remain long in the South, when their own
land was being devastated. They could not have
concentrated a force at any given point that would
have checked the headway of the advancing columns.
The result of such a campaign would have soon
raised the cry, in the North, for a sessation of hostilities. The Yanks could not have stood that kind
of warfare long, without making some kind of a
proposition for the adjustment of the difficulty.
Morgan's scheme was considered visionary, as he was
not a "West Pointer." From his experience in that
kind of warfare, he thought that it was the only way
the North could be made to feel the disastrous
effects of the war. General Morgan was a born
leader; a man of great natural military genius;
quick to perceive and prompt to act; he took in the
situation at a glance, and seldom failed to carry his
point. His efforts in the field, however, were greatly
retarded by too much "red tape." It does not follow that every one who has received a military
education should develop into a great captain, any
more than that every graduate of our leading col-
leges should turn out to be a Shakespeare, a Scott, or

a Byron. The world's history records but few startling military leaders.

A few days after reaching camp, I was ordered to
report to General Bragg's headquarters, at Tulahoma.
On presenting myself, the general informed me that
there was a wounded Federal officer, confined in the
hospital at Chattanooga, who fell into our hands at
the battle of Stone River, and had expressed a desire
to see me, if possible. Feeling it but a courtesy due
one soldier to another, General Bragg had granted
the permission.

When I reached Chattanooga, I presented my
papers to Colonel Stoaks, the commander of the post,
who received me courteously and offered to accompany me on my mission. We were not long in
reaching the hospital, where the wounded Federals
were located.

I found in Dr. Bemas, the surgeon in charge, an
old friend, who showed us the way to the officer's
ward, where, to my very great astonishment, who
should I find stretched out on one of the bunks, with
his head bound up in cloths but my friend of the
United States army, whom I had parted with at
Brownsville, on the Rio Grande, two years previous.
At first sight, I scarcely knew him. His hospital
garb was in striking contrast to the gaudy uniform
he wore when he stepped lightly on board the little
steamer, which bore him from the charmed spot in the
far West he seemed so reluctant to leave. I stopped beside his couch, and he recognized me at once and feebly
stretched forth his hand to grasp mine. As he did
so I thought I could see the mist gather in his eyes.

He expressed his gratification at my coming to him. We had been conversing but a short while when the doctor informed me that it would not be well for him to talk long at a time. I had a thousand things to talk to him about, but I was compelled to forego that pleasure until he grew stronger. The doctor informed me that he thought he would be better in a few days, as he was improving rapidly. He received every attention that was necessary for his comfort. Dr. Bemas was a Kentuckian and knew the young officer's family well. As I arose to start I reminded him that if there was anything I could do to alleviate his sufferings, he must not hesitate to call on me. He said: "I appreciate your kindness, and will avail myself of the offer." As we parted he exclaimed, "War is a terrible thing." On our way back to the colonel's quarters, I told him of our relationship to each other.

"It seems," he remarked, "that there is a little love affair mixed up with the matter." "Yes, a slight sprinkling of romance," I replied. The colonel seemed to take quite an interest in the young man and expressed a wish that he might get through the war all safe and be restored to the arms of his Mexican sweetheart.

Our conversation then drifted to the condition of the country and the state of the war. Kentucky, for a while, tried to maintain neutrality. She was very much divided in sentiment; a strong Union feeling prevailed throughout the State; family ties were rent asunder; brother was fighting against brother; and father against son; which caused bitter feuds. The people were compelled to take one side or the other, and the result was the blood of kindred, shed by kindred, stained the battle-fields. The bitterness engendered by the war, I am happy to say, has become almost entirely obliterated; and her gallant sons who wore the Gray and those who wore the Blue, have yielded to the inevitable and, in a measure, have become reconciled.

My visit to the bedside of my Yankee friend (at that time we called them all Yankees) were frequent. He continued to improve, and in a few days the doctor gave him permission to sit up part of the day and to talk as much as he liked. He had a " holy horror " of being sent to a Southern prison, and would frequently ask me if there was any way of avoiding it. I told him I thought there was ; at least I would make an effort to effect a special exchange, and on my return would confer with General Bragg about it ; this seemed to revive him very much.

It may appear strange to some who do not understand it, why I should take so much interest in one who was fighting against me. There was no personal animosity existing between the soldiers on either side. It was for PRINCIPLES we fought and not to gratify any petty revenge. Then again, this officer and I had been firm friends before the war. We frequently passed the time relating our adventures. He had been in many hard-fought battles, and had been twice promoted for gallantry on the field.

He had kept up a correspondence with his Mexican beauty, but the route was long and circuitous, and the letters were a long time in reaching him. He handed me a letter from her which he had received a few days before the battle occurred in which he had been wounded.   It was free from any sentimentality, was pure, chaste and elegant; just such a letter as I would suppose a lady of her intelligence would write. It was a long epistle and dwelt largely upon the political complications which were arising in Mexico. France was attempting to overthrow the then existing form of government and establish a monarchy. She had already landed troops on Mexican soil. Mexico was rallying her forces to resist the encroachment; every loyal citizen was called upon to do his duty.   The young lady's father and a younger brother had already gone to the front.   She was in great trouble, but took a philosophical view of the situation.   Her whole soul seemed to be absorbed in the welfare of her country and anxiety for those who were absent.   She made no attempt to conceal her attachment for her distant lover, who was fighting in a foreign land.

After I had finished reading the letter, I asked him what he thought of the situation in the " land of the cactus."   He replied that it was a gross violation of the " Monroe Doctrine," and something to which the United States would not submit.   As soon as she finished up the " little job " she had on hand at home, she would turn her attention in that direction.

"Then you think the North will succeed in this struggle," I asked.

"There is no doubt about it ; it is simply a question of time.   The whole South is in a state of siege.

Our armies by land and the navy by sea are maintaining a vigilant blockade."

Becoming animated, he went on to say : " While the heroic valor of your troops has never been excelled, they must, at last, yield to the overwhelming numbers we can bring against them. Our resources are inexhaustible. I have many friends in the Southern army, some of whom were my schoolmates, and for all of them I entertain the highest regard. Had I been a private citizen, living in my native State, I have no doubt that I would have cast my fortunes with the South. As it was, I debated the matter in my mind for some time before I reached a decision. I believe I am right in standing by the Constitution and the old flag. You believe to the contrary, and that is all the difference there is between us. I never would have drawn my sword to free the slaves. That was not the issue involved ; it was to prevent the disruption of the Union that prompted me to take side with the North. I believe the South should have been protected in her Constitutional rights, even if it had required an appeal to arms. If things had assumed that shape, I would have been with you. Secession and a dismemberment of the Union is what solidified the North. As matters now stand there is no alternative but to fight it out."

In the main I agreed with him, but said nothing.

"By the by," he exclaimed, " Is it possible to send a letter through the country to Mexico ? "

" It is," I replied, " We have a regular line of couriers established to Texas and extending on to the Rio Grande ; and that reminds me that I must go and prepare a letter, as a courier starts in the morning. "

" Very well," said he, " I will avail myself of the opportunity."

" Present my kind regards to the lady over the border, Captain, when you write," I remarked, as I bade him good-night.

" I shall be sure to do that, and I shall also inform her of the many acts of kindness you have done me, which I know will be duly appreciated."

The next day I informed my friend that as he was so much better, I would return to my command, and on the way would call on General Bragg and see what could be done in regard to an exchange.

The doctor told me that he was getting on as well as could be desired, and thought he could be removed in a few days.

When I reached General Bragg's headquarters I put the case before him. After a few moments reflection he complied with the request, and stated that he would send a flag of truce to the Federal lines in the morning, and I could accompany it if I so desired.

The next morning, with a white flag and a staff officer in charge of the necessary escort, we started on our mission of mercy. We reached the Federal lines after a ride of an hour, where our flag was received with all the formalities incident to such occasions. Our communication was transmitted to the commanding general, and we remained at the outposts to await developments, where we had a very pleasant chat for an hour with the Yankee officers. A reply was received, and on reaching Bragg's headquarters we were informed that everything was satisfactory, and that day a week hence had been designated for the exchange. I at once addressed a note to my friend, telling him that everything had been arranged for him to report to General Bragg at the appointed time, and that Colonel Stoaks had been instructed to make all the necessary arrangements for his transportation.

On the day appointed for the exchange I rode over to Bragg's quarters and accompanied the party to the Federal lines. The exchange was effected for a Confederate officer of equal rank.

When I bade my wounded friend good-bye, he remarked, as on a former occasion, "If we should at "any time recognize each other on the field, elevate "your gun, and I will do the same." "All right," I replied. He informed me that while confined in the hospital at Chattanooga the Confederate officers with whom he came in contact treated him with the utmost kindness, and seemed to avoid making any unpleasant allusion to the war. Colonel Stoaks, the commandant of the post, assisted him in getting his letters off all right, and extended many other acts of courtesy, for which he felt very grateful. He spoke in high terms of Dr. Bemas, the surgeon in charge, and regarded him as a noble, kind-hearted gentleman.

At one of our interviews, while he was in confinement, he seemed to be in quite a talkative mood, and related to me the occasion of his first meeting with the fair young Mexican beauty for whom he had formed so warm and ardent attachment. Her father was largely interested in silver mining in Northern Mexico. It was his custom to take his family and spend several weeks, during the summer, in the vicinity of his mines. There they could enjoy the exhilarating, pure mountain air, and indulge in the sport of hunting and fishing; could roam among the woods and hills, gathering wild flowers, and gaze with wonder and admiration upon the wild and picturesque scenery.

At the time of one of these summer outings it happened that our hero was stationed at one of the military posts on the upper Rio Grande. He had been out with a troop of cavalry in pursuit of a marauding band of Indians that had been annoying the settlers in that section for some time. He had followed them some distance into Mexico, but failed to come up with them. On his return he rode into one of the beautiful valleys of that region where there was a luxuriant growth of grass and a sparkling stream of water abounding in mountain trout. He decided to call a halt for a few days that they might recruit, the horses being considerably jaded after their long march. The lieutenant, while strolling along one evening near a mining camp in search of game, caught the sound of a female voice chanting a sweet Mexican song, accompanied by the soft strains of a guitar. At first he thought it was a mountain lass belonging to one of the camps, but after a moment's reflection he decided that the mellow cadence of that voice, blending with the soft evening breeze, betrayed culture not to be obtained in those mountain gorges. The delicate touch on the strings of the instrument was not by the hand of a novice. He remained stationary until the song was ended; then moving forward a few steps and turning an abrupt point of rocks, he beheld the object of his search, fair as the wreath of wild flowers which graced her raven hair. Discovering a stranger near, she arose from her reclining position like a startled fawn. But—

"Not his the form, nor his the eye,
That youthful maidens wont to fly."

He raised his cap, and with a graceful bow begged pardon for the abrupt intrusion, which was readily granted. He then told her of his wild and fruitless pursuit of the Indians, and how he came to stop in those enchanting regions. She said she was just on the point of returning to her father's camp, which was but a short distance away. He at once proffered to escort her, and she accepted with a refined and gentle courtesy. When they reached the camp her father greeted the stranger with a cordial welcome, and extended to the young gallant the hospitality of his hacienda, which was accepted, and he was delightfully entertained by the young lady; and the evening had far advanced when he arose to depart. His host invited him to spend several days with them and join in the mountain sports, which he accepted as freely as it was generously given; then bidding them good-night, started for his camp. It was quite late when he stretched himself on his pallet for his night's repose, for Cupid's dart had played sad havoc with his mental equilibrium. He arose bright and early the next morning and was soon off to his post, where he entertained his fellow-officers relating his somewhat romantic adventure.

It was not long before he applied for a few day's leave of absence, and soon found himself located at the pleasant retreat of the wealthy Spaniard, where he was entertained with the lavish hospitality so characteristic of the better class of Mexicans. Here he spent the most of his time in the mountains, hunting, fishing, and gathering wild flowers. On many of these rambles, the fair mountain beauty would accompany him, and they would return laden with trophies of the field, the brook and the chase.

It was beneath the shadow of those towering peaks and along the banks of those pure rippling streams, that tender emotions had sprung up between the two. Those emotions afterwards ripened into a pure and ardent attachment.

Summer was drawing to a close, and the time was approaching for the family to take their departure from that wild and enchanting spot to their winter home. A few days before they were to start, the lieutenant came to bid them adieu. It was a summer's night in the mountains; the pale moon had just risen above the cliffs and shed its soft and mellow light through the branches that overhung the precipices above; the two young lovers were seated on a moss-covered declivity of the rocks. They were silent for awhile; both were doubtless thinking of the separation that was soon to take place. He was the first to break the silence. He grasped her hand and told his love in such impassioned eloquence she could have no

doubt of its sincerity. It required but a gentle pressure of the hand to assure him that his love was re-
ciprocated. In a few days the family left for the
south.

The young lady was an only daughter and had full
charge of her father's household affairs, her mother
having been dead several years.

It was some time previous to the occurrence just related, that I formed the acquaintance of the young
lieutenant. I first met him on the frontier of Texas,
shortly after he graduated from West Point. We
were intimately associated in government affairs and
became warmly attached to each other. A few
months after the pleasant little episode just narrated,
the battery to which the young lieutenant was attached, was transferred to Brownsville (Fort Brown),
on the lower Rio Grande. There I met him as has
been related.

6 b g

CHAPTER X.

CAPTURE AND ESCAPE—ON BRAGG'S FLANKS—
FOURTH OHIO CAVALRY TRADING—MORGAN A
GOOD SPY—THE LION CATCHER CAUGHT—POOR
CHAMP FERGUSON—OUR WOMEN.

CAPTURE AND ESCAPE.

I will here give an incident which illustrates the
desperate chances taken by Confederate soldiers to escape prison.

If there was any one thing more than another for
which a Confederate had a holy horror, it was a Federal prison.

In the latter part of 1862, a portion of Morgan's
command was on a scout in the vicinity of the Hermitage, Jackson's old home, about nine miles from
Nashville, when they unexpectedly encountered the
Fourth Ohio cavalry. A charge was ordered, resulting in the capture of a captain and a lieutenant of
Morgan's command, who were taken to Nashville and
placed in the penitentiary. In a few days they were
ironed together and sent forward under guard to
Louisville, Ky. In Louisville they were placed in a
foul and loathsome dungeon, occupied by negroes,
thieves, deserters and vermin.

In this mundane hell these officers were confined,
whose only crime was the defending a principle
which they held dearer than life.

The captain addressed a courteous note to the
commandant of the post, politely requesting] that

officer to call at the prison, as he was in possession of important information he desired to communicate to him. The commandant was soon at the prison and was asked by the captain: "Is this the treatment you propose to accord to Confederate prisoners-of-war?"

The commandant was positive and very emphatic in his condemnation of the treatment of the Confederates, and had them immediately removed to proper quarters and ordered them furnished with everything necessary for their comfort. These changes were due to the fact that the commandant was an old army officer who understood his duty and his obligations, and a conscientious gentleman who enforced them.

After about a week's confinement in Louisville, these two officers were started by separate routes, for Northern prisons, the captain being taken by way of Indianapolis and the lieutenant by way of Cincinnati.

The routes taken suggest the reason; they knew that Morgan's men were apt to take desperate chances and that success was less likely to crown the efforts of one than the combined efforts of two daring, reckless men for escape.

But these two "Johnnies" had not the most remote idea of being shut up in a Yankee prison; consequently were always on the alert and ready to take advantage of even the scintilla of a chance, for there was but the toss of a biscuit between death and the horrors of a Federal prison.

The train bearing the captain came to a halt just

after dark, to take on a supply of water. At this time the captain was standing on the rear platform, talking with his guard; and as the engine began moving slowly forward, he made a desperate leap for liberty! His guard fired, but missed his aim and only accelerated the speed of the fleeing Confederate, who was soon lost to sight in the sheltering timber and darkness of the night.

After wandering about in an unknown wood until completely exhausted, the captain laid himself down beneath the spreading arms of a giant oak and was soon wrapt in profound slumber, oblivious of all the ills of his checkered life.

The sun was high in the heavens when the captain awaked, much refreshed, but a little hungry—the normal condition of all true Confederates. His position was distressingly perplexing. Here he was, free, but in the enemy's country, entirely unknown to him, without a cent of money, and in full Confederate Captain's uniform. What was he to do?

As evening came on his wanderings had brought him to an opening, in which he descried a well-to-do farm settlement. The time had arrived for decisive action, but what that should be had not been determined, when he saw a gentleman on horseback approaching.

The sight of the horse suggested a means of escape. Concealed in his boot-leg he had a pistol, which had escaped the Federal search; this he transferred to his coat-sleeve and awaited the man's approach.

The stranger saluted the captain with a smile and

remarked that he had the appearance of an escaped Confederate prisoner. To which the captain replied:

" You are correct, sir, and one who has tasted neither water nor food within twenty-four hours."

" Fortunately for you," replied the stranger, " you have fallen into friendly hands. I am what they style in this country a ' Copper-head ' or Southern sympathizer. Come along with me, and I will see what can be done to get you out of the country."

In reply to his questions the new-found friend informed the captain that he was in the State of Ohio and about ten miles from the small town of Xenia, and that the Southern sentiment was strong in that section.

The captain had surrendered to the kind stranger, who took him home with him, furnished him with a suit of citizen's clothes, a comfortable bed and generous food ; then, on the following morning accompanied the now transmogrified captain to Xenia, where he purchased for him a ticket to Cincinnati, saw him aboard the train and with a warm grasp of the hand congratulated him on his escape from a Federal prison, and bade him God-speed on his way back to Dixie.

On reaching Cincinnati the captain registered at the Burnett House.

In passing up the long flight of stone steps which leads to the entrance, who should he meet, face to face, but the lieutenant who was captured at the same time. The pleasure of that meeting can be imagined only by an old soldier.

In the quiet of their room they recounted their

adventures since they separated at Louisville. The lieutenant had escaped, as did the captain, by jumping from a train.

In Cincinnati they found friends who furnished them all the aid they required, which enabled them to supply all of their necessities, among other things a pair of good six-shooters. After dark they crossed over the Ohio and entered Covington, Ky., where they hired two good saddle-horses, ostensibly to take them to a wedding some miles in the country; this ruse was to give them time to get miles away before they would be followed.

The next morning at daylight they were sixty miles from Covington and their horses completely broken down; so they turned them loose, placed the saddles upon a fence and took to the woods, as a precaution.

About ten miles from where the horses were turned loose lived the father of one of Morgan's officers; for his house the Confederate officers made their way. In this neighborhood they found numerous friends, who supplied them with every means of getting out of the country, including fine Kentucky horses.

Nothing occurred before reaching the Confederate lines, save the every-day excitement in those regions, of running the gauntlet of the bushwhackers who infested every mountain pass in Kentucky and Tennessee.

The adventures narrated are but tame to some of the experiences of Confederates which, if given to the public, would equal in startling interest the most exciting romance ever written.

Our duties on the flank of Bragg's army were laborious. We were constantly on the move, exposed to all kinds of weather and out at all times of night, capturing Yankee forage trains, harassing their transportation and cutting off their pickets. Scarcely a day passed that we did not capture more or less prisoners.

The Fourth Ohio cavalry became as well acquainted in our camps as they were in their own. We had an understanding that when we captured any of their men we would exchange them on the field. The result was that we were passing them backward and forward every few days.

The boys kept up a lively little trade along the lines, in blankets, gum cloths, coffee and tobacco. They went so far, sometimes, as to swap horses. It was about the only chance we had to obtain "sure enough" coffee, except when we could capture it.

Our command subsisted for over two months on the generosity of the Yankee quartermasters. We would fight one day and trade the next.

While all this was going on Morgan was not inactive. He was ever on the watch, and at times, in various disguises, he would spend several days inside the Federal lines, always keeping himself thoroughly informed as to the movements of the enemy. At one time he remained one day and night in Nashville disguised as a Federal officer. At another time he passed inside the lines disguised as a countryman, with a load of produce, driving a single steer, and disposed of his load to the Federal soldiers at remunerative prices. He had also a jug of " mountain

dew" along, which he sold at a big profit. He not
only came back with his pockets well filled with
greenbacks, but with the information that a heavy
scout was to start out late in the afternoon for the
purpose of making a night attack upon his camp,
which gave ample time to make all preparations to
meet them.

We went out on the Nashville and Lebanon Pike,
near the old Jackson Hermitage, twelve miles from
Nashville; were distributed for some distance along
the road, covered by a dense growth of cedars, taking
our positions as quietly as possible, not a man being
allowed to speak. About 1 o'clock in the morning
the rattle of sabers and the tramp of horses broke the
stillness of the night. When they were well advanced along our lines the command "Halt!" was
given, and was repeated all along the lines with the
demand to surrender. We were in their front, along
their flank and in their rear. We had led them into
a trap, and there was no alternative but to surrender.
We captured the entire party without firing a gun.
There was over three hundred men, mounted on good
horses and well equipped. It was a big haul for one
night's operation.

The commanding officer was very much perplexed
as to how we became apprised of his design; but on
that point we remained *mum*.

Doubtless, while riding along at the head of his
column that night, the gallant Colonel had imagined
himself marching Morgan and his men through the
streets of Nashville as captives, while his name was
being heralded all over the land as the hero of Mor-

gan's capture. But all his bright prospects for rapid promotion had been nipped in the bud. Poor fellow! he fell, and as Moore has expressed it :

"'Twas ever thus from childhood's hours,
He'd seen his fondest hopes decay."

Our spies were ever watchful, always on the alert, keeping themselves well informed as to what was transpiring within the enemy's camps, which rendered it almost impossible for any movement to be made without our Generals being apprised of it in time. They were passing in and out of the Federal lines daily. One of the most daring and adroit of our spies was a man known as "Morgan's Pathfinder" (Champ Ferguson), a tall, dark-haired man with small, flashing black eyes, and somewhat stoop-shouldered. He carried a large white-handled bowie-knife in his belt, while a pair of "Navy six-shooters" always hung by his side. Everything about the man stamped him as one with whom it would not be safe to interfere, unless you had great advantage. He usually traveled by himself, possessing an accurate knowledge of all the paths through the mountains of Tennessee and Southern Kentucky. He was very reticent; at the same time he was a man of more than ordinary intelligence. He was living in Kentucky at the time the war broke out, near the border of Tennessee, where he had a comfortable home, was surrounded by an interesting family, and was regarded in the neighborhood as an exemplary citizen, and he, no doubt, would have remained so, had it not been for an incident that occurred about six months after hostilities commenced, which changed the current of his whole life.

While he was absent from home on one occasion a
band of notorious outlaws came to his house and demanded something to eat.   After finishing their meal
which had been so generously prepared they commenced robbing and plundering the house.   Not being satisfied with sacking the house they grossly
violated the ladies who had so generously furnished
them food.   While the mother was on her bended
knees pleading for her daughter, a beautiful girl of
sixteen, she was foully murdered: " No beast so
fierce but has some touch of pity "—these had none !

After committing most heinous atrocities these
fiends in human shape burned the house the better to
conceal their damnable crimes.   Ferguson learned
the facts from a little boy who was a short distance
from the house when the vile deeds were perpetrated,
and who upon hearing the screams of the ladies had
secreted himself in the bushes near by.

The grief-stricken husband and father took in the
situation at a glance, seated himself on a log and with
scalding tears bewailed his dreadful condition.   After
the first burst of grief had somewhat subsided he rose
to his feet, and with uplifted hands in the presence
of his God and over the ashes of his loved ones, he
took a vow that he would camp on the trail of these
devils incarnate who had brought such ruin and desolation to his home, and never would he cease to pursue and slay the demoniacal fiends as long as life
should last.

It was stated at that time by the very best of
authority, that first and last, that seventy-five or a
hundred of these marauders fell by his hands.   He

was not a regular attaché of Morgan's command, but rendered him valuable service and spent much of his time about his camps.

At one time Ferguson conducted the famous female spy, Belle Boyd, from Louisville, Kentucky, across the country on horse-back safely inside of our own lines.

Poor fellow! he died in Nashville, a few months after the war closed, broken in health and in spirits, "Unwept and unsung."

This limited sketch of a noted character is given in partial extenuation of his career, to make known the cruel deeds which drove him to desperation. While the rest of the civilized world will revolt at the methods he adopted to seek revenge, I am willing to cast the mantle of charity over his many deeds of blood, and submit his case to a higher tribunal for a final adjudication. The regular soldiers disapproved of the course he pursued, and Morgan would frequently remonstrate with him in regard to the merciless character of his retaliation. He would make but one reply: "General, place yourself under similar circumstances, and you will think otherwise."

Our spies were everywhere; in the Northern cities, within the Federal lines, close about army headquarters; and, sometimes, they were in close proximity, when important consultations were being held, between the President and his cabinet; and information gained, would be rapidly transmitted within our lines. By that means our Generals were apprised in due time, of nearly every important movement of the enemy. Females, as a general thing, made the best.

spies. They created less suspicion and could adopt a greater variety of disguises; sometimes as nurses in the Federal hospitals; at others, distributing tracts among the soldiers; and, not infrequently, would they assume the character of a "Sister of Charity." Their calling was dangerous; the penalty, if caught, was death; still they would take the risk, in their devotion to the cause of the South.

History records no instance of purer patriotism, or a more self-sacrificing devotion, than was manifested by the ladies of the South, during the great struggle. They could be found in the hospitals; about the camps; on the field, mingling with the dead and wounded; in fact, everywhere that her loving heart, her brain and her hands could, in any way, contribute to the relief of the Southern soldiers, and the cause of the South. Her attentions were not exclusively confined to the Southern soldiers. Many a sick and wounded Federal could testify to her kindness. I recall one instance, where a woman's soft and gentle nature was most strikingly displayed: A bright, smooth-faced Yankee boy was brought to one of our hospitals, mortally wounded, who lived but a few hours after his wounds were dressed. A Southern lady was passing; she stopped for a moment and looked upon his youthful face, cold in death; then bent over his lifeless form with the remark, "I'll kiss him for his mother;" and imprinted that warm token of affection upon his cold and clammy brow. How many such unheralded acts, done in pure sympathy, were performed during the war, will never be known. However, the eye of Him who gave his precious life, on

the cross of Calvary, is in all such deeds of love and
mercy, and they will be rewarded. The women of
the South worked for the soldiers during the war.
Too much cannot be said in praise of their noble, self-
sacrificing devotion. In every city, village, hamlet,
valley and plain, they made cloth and clothing;
scraped lint and prepared bandages; prepared dainties
for the sick and wounded; and wrote words of cheer .
to the boys in the field. These things showed the
soldier boys that our noble women were thinking of
them. Like ministering angels they went to the hospitals; and, though in pain—often in the face of
death, the soldier turned on his cot to bless them
as they passed. They took down the words of the
dying husband, ere his spirit took its flight, and sent
them to the widowed one, far away; they cheered the
fainting boy into life; and the touch of their soft
hands, was as a healing balm to the burning, fevered
brow on which they were placed. Kind words for
the despondent; gentle acts for those racked by pain,
and tears, as pure and sympathetic as the angels', for
those who lay on a soldier's bier. It was owing, in
a great measure, to her words of cheer and acts of
encouragement, that our soldiers were stimulated to
deeds of bravery which stand unequaled in the annals
of war.

CHAPTER XI.

BRAGG AT CHATTANOOGA—MORALE OF THE ARMY
—MORGAN IN OHIO—HIS CAPTURE AND ESCAPE—
RAID INTO TENNESSEE—MORGAN BETRAYED AND
KILLED—DUKE IN COMMAND—"CERRO GORDO"
WILLIAMS SENT INTO TENNESSEE—FIGHT AT
SALT WORKS—OUR FIRST INTRODUCTION TO THE
"BROTHER IN BLACK" AS A SOLDIER.

Bragg at this time was at Chattanooga, making preparations for another big battle, that he might the more thoroughly put things in a proper shape for paving his retrograde movements with dead bodies.

The army under Lee held their position and were winning victories against overwhelming odds. Our army in Tennessee was losing ground every day. The soldiers had lost all confidence in their commander.

While these discouraging elements were at work, the Confederate Congress dealt a blow to the South, from which she never recovered. They passed an act exempting all men from the army who could control property to the amount of a few hundred dollars. The cry was at once "a rich man's war and a poor man's fight;" and the result was thousands of deser-tions. At the same time, their confidence in their immediate leaders was not shaken, and they were willing to press on and continue the struggle to the bitter end. Disaster had followed disaster in rapid succession. Vicksburg had fallen, with a loss of thirty-seven thousand prisoners captured, and over ten thousand killed and wounded. This was a terri-

ble blow to the Confederacy, cutting off all direct
communication with the States west of the Mississippi river. Morgan had gone on a raid into the
enemy's territory, north of the Ohio river, which resulted in the capture of over half of his command,
reducing Bragg's cavalry force to a minimum. The
Federal commander, Rosecrans, had taken advantage
of this and made an effort to dislodge Bragg from
Chattanooga.

Morgan crossed the Ohio river at Brandenburg, by
pressing two steamboats into service. He then made
a circuit around Cincinnati, not deeming it expedient
to attempt a capture of the city, owing to the demoral-
izing effect it would have upon his army. He moved
on to Buffington's Island, where he found the river
past fording, something that had not been known to
occur, at that season, for years. This delay enabled
the gunboats to come up and command the ford and
compel him to capitulate. Morgan admitted afterwards that he made a great mistake in keeping so
close to the river. He was under the impression that
if he had headed north, burned bridges, cut telegraph
wires, he could, by rapid marches, have reached the
lakes; swept around through Eastern Ohio and Western Pennsylvania, and passed out through West Virginia. In this event his expedition might have proved
a success. The only effect it produced, however, was
to give the people a big scare.

Morgan and the officers who were captured with
him were taken to Columbus and placed in the Ohio
penitentiary. This was considered one of the strong-
est prison-houses in the North. After a confinement

of four months, Morgan, with seven of his companions, made his escape, which was effected by mining under the wall of one of the cells on the ground floor of the main building. It was a long and tedious operation, but in the end, those bold spirits accomplished their object, and once more enjoyed the air of freedom. They scaled the outer wall with strips of bedclothing twisted into a rope. Once outside, they separated, with the understanding that they would make their way back to the Confederate lines as best they could.

It was not until morning when the warden of the prison came around to let them out for breakfast that their escape was made known. When it was fully realized that they were gone, the news spread in every direction, and the wires were kept hot. The whole country was aroused; everybody for miles around was on the alert, private houses were searched, where there was the most remote suspicion that the inmates were in sympathy with the rebels. Barns were ransacked, old wells were looked into, dry goods boxes were turned over, and it is said they even went so far as to turn over big rocks, thinking Morgan might have turned into a gopher and was burrowing in the ground. Men were stationed at short intervals all along the Ohio river for miles to watch, with instructions to "wink but one eye at a time." Notwithstanding all their vigilance, Morgan, with his daring comrades, landed in due time inside the Confederate lines.

There was an impression at the time, and it exists in the minds of many to this day that Morgan received aid from outside, which enabled him to make his escape. That impression is erroneous. Captain

Hines, of the Ninth Kentucky (my regiment), was the man who planned the escape and carried it to a successful termination.

After the war, Captain Hines became circuit judge of one of the districts of Western Kentucky and died several years ago. He was a gallant soldier and a gentleman of varied accomplishments.

Soon after Morgan returned from prison he gathered about him a few of his trusty followers, started into Kentucky on a recruiting expedition and brought out several hundred men.

At Greenville, a small town in East Tennessee, he was betrayed and surprised about daylight at the house of a Mrs. Williams, where he was making his head-quarters, by a federal force. The house was surroun-ded and he ordered to surrender, which he refused to do, and a desperate hand-to-hand fight ensued. He fell, mortally wounded and died before he could be removed.

On that spot, went out the life of one of the South's most sagacious, daring and gallant leaders. His bril-liant military career had made him famous through-out all parts of the world. At that time he was bet-ter known than any other cavalry officer in the Con-federate service.

Morgan was hampered to a great extent in his ope-rations by a spirit of envy that existed among a cer-tain class of army officers. They looked upon his movements with a jealous eye and would quietly in-terpose obstacles which would frustrate his plans. At one time he was on the point of sending in his resig-nation, but his friends prevailed on him to abandon the idea. Notwithstanding the venom with which his enemies pointed their shafts hurled at him; when the future historian comes to recount his many daring exploits his name will stand out as one of the foremost chieftains who figured in the great struggle for Southern independence.

> "He pitched his tent on fame's eternal camping-ground,
> And no foul aspersions can sully his fair renown."

General Basil Duke succeeded to the command. He was a dashing officer and an accomplished gentleman. He was formerly Morgan's trusted lieutenant and contributed largely to the fame of our lost hero. General Duke now stands at the head of the legal fraternity in Kentucky.

General Joseph Wheeler was in command of all the cavalry forces attached to the Tennessee army.

The Federals were pressing us on all sides. General John S. Williams ("Cerro Gordo," as the boys called him on account of his bravery in that noted battle in Mexico), was sent with a detachment of cavalry into East Tennessee to check the advance of a Federal move in that direction. My own regiment was attached to that command. We succeeded in our mission, but a force had in the meantime, gotten in our rear and we were compelled to make our way out through West Virginia, where the largest salt-works in the Confederacy were located, and which were of an immense advantage to the South, as they furnished most of the salt consumed by the armies. The Washington authorities, realizing this fact, sent a force of six thousand men, consisting of infantry, cavalry and artillery (including one brigade of negroes) to destroy them. They were all under the command of General Burbridge. Our command consisted of twelve hundred men.

The salt-works were located at the little mountain town of Saltville.

We had reached a point forty miles from there and had decided to remain and recruit our horses for a few days, little dreaming that we would meet the enemy in that section. We were just fairly settled in camp when about four o'clock in the evening, a courier came dashing up to General Williams's headquarters with a dispatch, stating that a heavy force was moving across the mountains in the direction of Saltville, and we were urged to come at once to the relief of the little band of "home guards," stationed at the works for their protection.

"Boots and saddles" was sounded, and just as the sun had passed the limit of the western horizon our columns moved out. We were put on a forced march and reached the place at day break, and got there none too soon, for Burbridge had come up and was forming his lines in the valley below for an attack. General Williams commenced at once to make hasty preparations to give him a warm reception. He dismounted most of his men, who, with the militia, he stretched along the crest of the hills, which were covered with a small undergrowth which concealed from the enemy our real strength. Saltville is located on an eminence and commands a remarkably fine view of the surrounding country, which is hilly and broken and difficult of access. Burbridge approached from the valley below in three lines of battle with the ne-

gro brigade forming the front line. We had in all,
about fifteen hundred men to meet this tremendous
odds. The Ninth Kentucky regiment remained
mounted with orders to charge whenever we saw the
enemy giving way.

Our lines were so extended that they amounted
scarcely to a good skirmish line. The four pieces of
artillery, which we found at the salt-works, were
placed in a commanding position and concealed from
the view of the enemy. Our men were instructed not
to fire a gun until "the whites of the enemy's eyes"
were distinctly visible. On they came, the darkies in
front. This was the first time that our command had
ever met the "colored brother" in battle. They
marched up in perfect order as if on dress parade.
The orders of the officers were plainly audible. Their
battle-cry was: "Remember Fort Pillow and take no
prisoners." This gave our men to understand what
they might expect if they fell into their hands.

It was not long before the darkies' eyes shown out
like a long line of Waterbury watches. The signal
was given to open fire and a deadly volley was
poured into their faces. This checked their advance
for a moment. They returned the fire with but little effect. The engagement soon became general. Our
artillery did splendid execution. It was not long before their lines began to waver; then they turned and
fled. They could no longer withstand the deadly fire
from our guns. In vain did their officers try to rally
them.

At this point the mounted men were ordered to
charge—and they charged home! The enemy were

panic-stricken, resulting in a complete rout. The ground was covered with dead and wounded men, knapsacks and canteens. Our victory was complete. Three thousand prisoners fell into our hands, together with a large number of wagons, guns and a quantity of army stores.

Burbridge, with a portion of his command, escaped into Kentucky. Our horses were too much jaded-- in fact were worn out—from the previous night's march, so we could not follow him.

The advantage of this victory to the South could hardly be estimated at that time. We had saved from destruction one of the largest salt-works in the Confederacy.

I have been somewhat minute in the description of this battle, from the fact that I have never seen mention of it in print. Like many other engagements of like character, it has been lost sight of, while many other brilliant victories have been graphically described which only resulted in the loss of thousands of our brave soldiers, without being of any practical benefit. I have no reliable data at this late date to refer to in order to estimate our loss in the battle of Saltville, as it was then called.

After the battle we returned to our camp, where we remained for a few days to let our men and horses rest. It was in a settlement of Dunkards, a peculiar religious sect (of Quakers), who were opposed to war, but we were treated very kindly by them.

CHAPTER XII.

AT CHATTANOOGA—LETTERS—ONE FROM MEXICO
—MAIL COURIERS—ROSECRANS ATTEMPTS TO
FLANK BRAGG—HE EVACUATES CHATTANOOGA—
BATTLE OF CHICKAMAUGA—MISSIONARY RIDGE
—THE RETREAT—BATTLE OF RINGGOLD GAP—IN
WINTER QUARTERS—THOUGHTS ON THE CONDI-
TIONS, NORTH AND SOUTH.

After a few days' rest in the fertile valleys of West
Virginia, we received orders to move. The rich
products of the fields were so abundant it was with
some reluctance we left the "Flesh-pots" of that
delightful region. That portion of Virginia had suffered very little from the ravages of war, as it was
removed from the scene of active hostilities.

A soldier is nothing more than a machine, and
must move at the word of command; therefore we
took up our march, over mountain, hills and valleys,
back to the army of Tennessee. Nothing occurred
to disturb our progress except now and then a lone
shot from some concealed bushwhacker who attempted
to obstruct our passage through some narrow gorge.
We reached the command in due time and found the
Federal forces in close proximity to Bragg, at Chattanooga.

The same routine of duty presented itself, such as
picketing, scouting and annoying the enemy's flanks.

The first place for which we made a break was
army headquarters, for letters. If there is any one
thing more than another that tends to revive the

spirits of a soldier it is the receipt of those little missives of affection and cheer from the dear ones at home. Nestling in the package that was handed to me was a letter from the far-off border of Mexico, addressed in a delicate female hand. It had traveled a long distance, and owing to the disturbed condition of the country, had been a long time on the way. I returned to camp much revived, but many wore a look of disappointment, having received no tidings from their dear home circles.

Seated beneath the branches of a towering oak, with eager expectations, I began to devour the contents of the package. There were a number of letters from friends and relatives; and while it had been a long time since they had been written, they gladdened my heart with the many tender messages of love and sympathy they contained, as if they had been written but an hour before.

The letter from Mexico was the last one I opened. It was written in Spanish and in a plain, legible hand, and ran thus:

"My Kind Friend:—I received a letter a few
" days ago from my friend, Lieutenant ———, post-
" marked Chattanooga, Tenn., in which he gave me
" a sad, but thrilling account of his capture and con-
" finement in a hospital, and, with great warmth of
" feeling, mentioned the many attentions you had
" paid him while suffering from a dangerous wound.
" I scarcely know how he will ever repay you for the
" many acts of kindness so generously bestowed. Oh,
" how I longed to be there that I, in my feeble way,
" might take some of the burden off your hands in
" ministering to his wants in the hour of his great af-

" fliction ; for you have doubtless been apprised of the
" relationship existing between us. Oh, these terri-
" ble wars ! It occurs to me that they are but relics
" of barbarism. It is strange indeed, at this age of
" the world, that some milder methods are not adopted
" to settle national disputes without mangling and
" slaughtering each other on the gory field. In my
" judgment, it is a serious reflection upon our boasted
" civilization. My anxiety is rendered doubly severe
" from the fact that father and brother have responded
" to their country's call. Our own fair land is threat-
" ened soon to be crimsoned with blood. I am left
" to look after matters at home. The only consola-
" tion I find in my greatest anxiety and mental de-
" pression is when I retire to my private closet, rosary
" in hand, and silently commune with the Virgin
" Mary and implore her to intercede for the safety of
" kindred and friends, so far away and surrounded by
" so many perils."   .   .   .

From the general tenor of her letter, I would in-
fer that the bent of her inclinations were with the
South in the great struggle ; at the same time she expressed a warm sympathy for the soldiers on both
sides.

The better class of Mexicans are a proud, haughty
and chivalrous people, entirely free from any taint of
puritanical fanaticism. They adhere strictly to their
primitive customs, social, domestic and religious.
They are slow to take up new ideas and adopt new
methods. Their country is as lovely as ever the sun
shone upon ; rich in minerals and agricultural products. No wonder they were aroused when France
tried to establish an Empire on Mexican soil, and
plant a foreign Prince upon her throne.

The young lady informed me that her father was

on the staff of General Escobeda, an officer who endeared himself to the Mexican people by his gallant act at the beautiful city of Queretaro. In this stronghold, the Emperor, Maximilian, had taken refuge. Escobeda besieged the place, and, with two of his staff, captured the monarch, Maximilian, who was tried by courtmartial, condemned, and shot. This restored that beautiful land to her brave and patriotic sons.

When I had finished the young lady's charming epistle, I laid down upon my blanket and soon dropped off to sleep. How long I slept, I know not, but when I awoke, the sun was just sinking behind the hills.

My mind had wandered back to the time when this blessed land of ours was free from turmoil, strife and blood; when the white-winged messenger of Peace hovered over a hapy, prosperous and contented people, with no thought that "grim-visaged war" would soon disturb the peaceful avocations of life.

After a hard night's ride in pursuit of a Federal scouting party, I procured a little Confederate writing paper, from one of the boys, and a small quantity of ink, that had been adulterated to such an extent that it was scarcely visible; then with a split stick, as a substitute for a pen, and a camp kettle for a desk, I entered upon the pleasing task of replying to the letters I had received.

The couriers detailed to transmit our mails to and from the trans-Mississippi department, were provided with a small bottle of combustible fluid and a few matches, so that, in the event that there was any dan-

ger of falling into the enemy's hands, letters might
quickly be destroyed.   It rarely occurred, however,
that one of them was captured, for they were shrewd,
brave and determined men.   They traveled on horseback
and were provided with relays, at intervals, all along
the route.   The most difficult obstruction they had
to encounter, was the passage of the Mississippi river.
There they were sometimes detained for several days.
Small boats were kept concealed in out of the way
places, at short distances from the river.   The passage
was usually effected during the night.   Sometimes
ladies would accompany these couriers, either on their
way to the bedside of some sick, or wounded soldier,
or returning with important dispatches for the Government.

Could the numerous adventures of these brave and
trusty men be written, it would read like a thrilling
romance.

While this pleasing episode of receiving and writing letters was going on, we were on the eve of one of
the most sanguinary battles of the war.   As I stated
in the outset of these sketches, there will be no
attempt to enter into minute details of great battles.
These have all been written up, time and time again.
I shall only attempt to give the outline and the result
of such engagements.   Bragg occupied Chattanooga ;
Rosecrans had secured a crossing of the Tennessee
river, by capturing Bridgeport, Ala.   He then pushed
forward two army corps, under Thomas and McCook,
across Sand Mountain and Lookout Mountain.   This
move placed Bragg's army at Chattanooga, in a peril-

ous position, and his communications were seriously threatened.

As Bragg always looked well to his rear, he, without delay, evacuated Chattanooga, and posted his army facing the mountains, through which the Federals were moving to his rear. For about ten days, there was skirmishing and some sharp fighting. About this time, Gen. Forrest defeated a large cavalry force near Ringgold, and captured a large number of prisoners.

The two armies fought shy of each other. Rosecrans occupied the north bank of the Chickamauga creek, the Confederates the south side.

Along the banks of that little stream, stood the invincible hosts of Bragg; and on the opposite bank was drawn up the most magnificently equipped army the North had ever sent into the field. It numbered more than 64,000 men, while Bragg was confronting them with a few over 33,000 men, badly equipped, badly clothed, and no pay—the Confederate money was considered worthless. This discrepancy in numbers placed the numerical advantage of the two armies, almost two to one in favor of the Federals. Soon the air would be filled with sulphurous smoke, and the banks of the little "river of death," covered with the dead and dying.

The first gun was fired, in the great battle of Chickamauga, September 18th, 1863. It occurred at a point known at that time as Reed's Bridge.

A detachment of Federal cavalry had been sent to destroy the bridge. They were met by a party of Confederates, who were guarding the position. The

Federals were repulsed and driven back in confusion
and then the struggle began. It was desperate and
bloody in the extreme. Never did troops fight with
more heroic courage, than did the men on both sides.
All during the day the Confederates had more than
held their own. The Federals had contested every
inch of ground with stubborn tenacity, until darkness
veiled the bloody scene, when both armies rested on
their arms for the night.

The next morning the battle opened with renewed
vigor, both sides refusing to yield. About 10 o'clock
Bragg was reinforced by Longstreet's corps. A
rebel yell went up which shook the very base of old
Lookout when Longstreet's corps plunged into the
fight. The Federals could not withstand the shock
of "Old Ironsides" (Longstreet) and his veteran
legions, whose banners had waved over many a victorious field. Rosecrans's army was soon routed and
in full retreat.

Had it not been for a desperate stand made by
Thomas, on Snodgrass Hill, the entire Federal army
would have been captured on the field. The three
pontoon bridges crossing the Tennessee river were
packed and jammed with fleeing Federal soldiers!
They resisted every effort of their officers to rally
them. Some of them did not stop short of the Ohio
river.

Here Bragg made a fatal mistake. Longstreet
plead with him to push on that night and complete
his victory. How unfortunate it was for the South
that Longstreet was not in command of that army!

While it was a crushing defeat to the Federals, it

was of no advantage to the South, only in evidencing the valor of her sons. We captured in the two days' fighting over 10,000 prisoners, 60 cannon, and a large amount of stores. It was difficult to ascertain the exact losses in men. Some estimate it at over 26,000 in killed and wounded on both sides.

After the battle our forces occupied Missionary Ridge and Lookout Mountain. From these elevated positions we had a commanding view of Chattanooga, and of the beautiful Tennessee river for miles.

General Wheeler, with a large cavalry force, was sent to the rear of Rosecrans's army, to harass his communication along the Nashville and Chattanooga railroad. The writer, with the 9th Kentucky and a detachment of Tennessee cavalry, was ordered to go to Lookout Valley, on the opposite side of the mountain, keep up a line of pickets along the bank of the Tennessee river as far down as Bridgeport, twenty miles below, and report to General Longstreet daily, in person, any movement of the enemy in that direction. Longstreet occupied Bragg's extreme left, which extended to the top of the mountain. Our duties were exceedingly laborious and very trying, owing to the extended scope of country we were compelled to cover with such a limited number of men.

I stated to General Bragg the difficulties in the way, and the impossibility to prevent a crossing should the enemy attemt to force one. He said: "Do the best you can, and I will send you more men as soon as they can be spared." This impressed me with the idea that it was a stroke of very bad generalship on the part of Bragg, to leave so important a line exposed to the incursions of the enemy without an adequate force to protect it, particularly so, when the enemy, in heavy force, was in my front. Besides the heavy guard duty we had to perform there were a number of bushwhackers and deserters in the mountains, whom we were compelled to look after.

To report to General Longstreet I was compelled to pass around the point of Lookout Mountain exposed to the fire of a Federal battery on the top of Moccason Heights, on the opposite side of the river, which covered the passage-way to Longstreet's headquarters. The Federals never failed to pay their compliments from that frowning eminence, in the shape of a few ten-inch shells, every time any one passed.

The exposed point was but a short distance, and always covered at full speed.

If I am not mistaken in time—I have no other data than memory to rely on—it was about ten days from the time we entered the valley that the Federals presented themselves on the opposite bank of the river with two sections of artillery, and, as I had predicted, effected a crossing and drove us from the valley.

We ascended Lookout Mountain by a bridle way, which we found very difficult to traverse, the men having to dismount and lead their horses.

About this time General Longstreet was sent to Knoxville for the purpose of reducing that point, which resulted in a failure. Walthall's brigade took Longstreet's place on Lookout Mountain.

Bragg's army was becoming weaker every day, by

numerous desertions and the great oversight in sending away so many of his best troops.

Grant, who had succeeded to the command of the Federal forces at Chattanooga, was receiving large reinforcements and making stupendous preparations for an advance; to hit the wedge another blow, which would rend the Confederacy in twain.

It did not require the experienced eye of a military expert to see 'that it was a ruinous policy to weaken so small an army in the face of an enemy that was every day augmenting his strength.

On the night of November 24th Hooker's corps succeeded in gaining the summit of Lookout Mountain, where he engaged Walthall, whose force numbered only about *fifteen hundred men*. After a stubborn and persistent resistance for several hours, Walthall retired in good order, before that vastly superior force, and reformed on Bragg's left, along the crest of Missionary Ridge.

On the morning of the 25th the fight opened all along the line, which extended over twelve miles. Bragg had fearful odds to contend against; his army was scarcely 35,000 men, while Grant brought into action on that eventful day, over 65,000 of the best equipped soldiers the North had ever sent to the field.

The evolutions of the Federals, as they moved from Chattanooga and formed on the plain below the Ridge, presented the grandest military display the eye ever beheld! It had more the appearance of a great dress parade, than an army forming for a desperate conflict; and as one of our men who viewed the great panorama in the valley below, remarked afterwards: "I

"stood firm until Grant rode out in front, on his
"splendid charger, and gave that celebrated order :
"' Attention word! Forward United States Bat-
"talion!' then I left."

The onslaught was terrific! Grant had with him
a number of leaders of marked ability ; and I don't
suppose any one ever questioned the fact that Grant
was far superior to Bragg as a military strategist.
Any one standing on the Ridge and viewing that vast
host moving to the attack, in such perfect order, would
naturally conclude that the Confederates would be
swept from the field, like straws before the blast !
Such was not the case, however.

The assault was made all along the lines, with the
impetuous daring and bravery so characteristic of an
army of determined men.

The invincible Cleburne, who occupied the right of
the Confederate line, received the first shock, and
right nobly did he hurl it back! his artillery cutting
broad swaths in their ranks. Three times they rallied
and renewed the assault, only to meet the same fate.

Sometimes the lines were so close Cleburne's men
were compelled to club their guns to beat them back.
Cleburne held his lines and captured seven stands of
colors.

After several hours' hard fighting, it did seem, notwithstanding the tremendous odds against us, that we
would hold our line in spite of them ; but we were
doomed to disappointment. The enemy had discovered a weak point near our left center, and made a
break for it, rending the air with enthusiastic cheers !
The ever-watchful eye of Hardee discovered the

breach in time, threw a portion of his command across
the ridge, and effectually checked them, and, no doubt,
saved Bragg's army from annihilation.

This opportune movement of Hardee's held the
Federals in check and gave Bragg a chance to withdraw his forces with but little confusion.

Some accounts of this "battle of the clouds,"
written from a Northern standpoint, have put it down
as a complete rout of Bragg's army. Had such been
the fact, there is no doubt but that the intrepid and
sagacious commander of the Federals would have
pushed on and captured Bragg's entire army; on the
contrary, Grant was very slow to move along that
line; only slight demonstrations being made the next
day. Bragg secured his very large wagon-train and
withdrew his army to a place of comparative safety.

As a participant in the battle of Missionary Ridge,
I have no wish to add to, or take from, the combatants,
on either side. I simply desire to give to the world a
clear, unvarnished statement of facts, as they occurred,
under my own observation.

As a portion of the unwritten history of the operations, subsequent to and immediately preceding the
battle, I will state that the writer was in command of
all the cavalry attached to Bragg's army at that time;
which was composed of separate detachments, which
did not accompany General Wheeler into Tennessee.
During the battle we occupied (dismounted) a position on the extreme right of Cleburne's lines and
were in the hottest of the fight.

A great mistake was made in sending the bulk of
the cavalry so far away when it might have been of

8 bg

so much service at that critical moment. Why was
Longstreet sent away!

On the evening after the battle, I started to look
for Bragg, that I might receive orders. I found him
about dark, in a small room at Chickamauga Station,
consulting a map of Georgia, with his chief of staff,
and I informed him that I had come for orders. He
asked me how many men I had. "Not over five hundred," I replied. He appeared somewhat astonished,
and asked where the balance were. I told him I pre-
sumed they were with General Wheeler, in Tennessee.
That seemed to annoy him; but he directed me to
proceed to a bridge on the Chickamauga, about five
miles distant, in the direction the Federals were approaching, and to destroy it; then to fall in the rear
of the infantry and cover their retreat.

We proceeded to within half a mile of the bridge.
There we ascertained that Hooker's whole corps had
crossed the bridge and gone into camp there. We
returned at once to report the situation, but found the
little station deserted; not a soldier was in sight. My
convictions were more than verified; Bragg fell far
short of being a great General.

We moved on in the direction we supposed our army
had taken. It was a bitter cold night, and the men
were suffering very much.

In an hour's time we came up with the rear guard
of General Gist's South Carolina Brigade. I rode to
the head of his column and reported to General Gist
what had taken place; how we came to be there, and
asked for orders. He thanked me very kindly, and
seemed much gratified to know that he had some-

cavalry in his rear. He directed me to take the place of his rear-guard and look after some Federal cavalry that had been annoying him, at intervals, up to that time. With the exception of one sharp little brush with them, they gave us no further trouble during the night.

It was a fearful night's march, and one long to be remembered by our cold, wet and hungry soldiers; the most of whom had not tasted food for three days.

While passing a defile, with a mountain on one side and the dark sluggish waters of the Chickamauga on the other, the horses attached to one of the batteries became so weak that they could pull their load no further. I took pity on the poor brutes and ordered the guns pitched into the stream. Four beautiful twelve-pound brass pieces were thrown into the river that night, and I have never heard that they were recovered. The water was quite deep and I have no doubt they are there to this day.

We reached Ringgold, a small town on the Western & Atlantic Railroad, about daylight. Here we found plenty of forage and provisions. We had not seen anything of the Yanks for some time; so I informed General Gist that I would stop for a while and refresh my men and horses. Not deeming it prudent to remain long in that locality, General Gist pushed on with his command.

The Yankees were quite obliging, for they did not put in an appearance for two hours. This gave us ample time for rest and to feed. At the expiration of that time our pickets reported Hooker's whole corps advancing in the direction of Ringgold. Hav-

ing no desire to exchange compliments with that
gentleman at that time, we moved along in the direction of Ringgold Gap.

Here we found General Cleburn in line of battle, with sixty pieces of artillery masked just inside
of the gap. He told me to pass on through his
lines, dismount my men, and form on his right; and
that he would try to "salivate them," when they came
up. We had not long to wait. Soon the head of
Hooker's columns came in full view. They were
flushed with their recent victory and came forward
with a rush and a whoop, thinking, no doubt, that
they would carry everything before them. Not a gun
was fired by our men until they got within fifty yards
of our lines.

I will here insert a short and very correct account
of the immediate battle, as taken from the "Mountain
Campaigns in Georgia." I take pleasure in stating
that the author's account is correct, *as far as it goes:*

" They made a determined attack upon the Confed-
" erates at all points. The fighting in the ravine
" and the counter ravine, at the northern end of the
" short ridge, extending from the pass several hun-
" dred yards, parallel to the railroad was very des-
" perate and bloody. The assaulting columns made
" some progress up the side of the ridge when the
" fire from the Confederate lines became so destructive
" and the rolling of huge rocks down the mountain
" slope threw the assailants into such confusion, and
" inflicted such loss that they were compelled to give
" over the attack. Hooker's forces then fell back

"through the town of Ringgold, burning it as they
" departed."

"Fighting Joe" had got his dose. He took himself back to Chattanooga, feeling not quite so much
elated as when he passed over the same road a few
hours before.

This engagement put a check to any further operations in that quarter, for several months.

The Federal army went into winter quarters at
Chattanooga, and the Confederate army, what was
left of it, went into quarters at Dalton. The cavalry
under General Wheeler occupied Tunnel Hill, a small
town about seven miles north of Dalton. The section of country between Chattanooga and Dalton
was " neutral ground." There were, however, frequent hostile meetings between scouting parties of
both armies, during the winter.

CHAPTER XIII.

BRAGG RELIEVED—JOHNSTON SUCCEEDS HIM—
REJOICING AMONG THE TROOPS—IMPROVEMENT
IN THE ARMY—CONDITION OF THE COUNTRY.

Bragg had made his last move on the military chess-board of the Confederacy, so far as related to the army of Tennessee. He was a brave and efficient subordinate officer, and I hope I may not be charged with doing an injustice to his memory, when I say that, as commander of an army in the field, he was a failure. That seemed to be the verdict of all with whom I conversed at the time; and the impartial historian must so record it.

There was great rejoicing in the army when it became known that Bragg had been relieved and General Joseph E. Johnston had been appointed to succeed him.

The soldiers, when Johnston took command, were greatly dispirited. They felt that all their victories, which had cost so much blood and so many lives, and the heroic sacrifices they had made for the cause had been but bubbles on the water.

General Johnston came to the army with a military prestige, second to no officer in either army. The soldiers had the utmost confidence in him. He inspired new hope. His influence was soon felt throughout the whole country. Deserters were coming in constantly. The morale of the army was greatly improved, and his forces were being augmented every day.

Little hope was entertained at that time of final success, unless some unforeseen event should occur to change the whole status of the army.

Our armies could cope successfully with the Federals on the field and win great battles against vastly superior numbers. Brilliant victories, however, went for naught. There was no encouraging outlook. The dark cloud of defeat, like a funeral pall, was fast settling over the South. Our splendid armies in Virginia, which we had looked to with so much hope, were gradually melting away. The West was slowly yielding before the advancing tread of the northern hosts. The wedge was entering the very heart of the Confederacy, and was being driven home. The territory over which both armies had passed was a desolate waste. The poor, trembling, bleeding South was held in the grasp of that blazing monster, War! Her fertile fields and lovely homes were fast becoming blackened spots on the surface of her once fair domain. Thousands of her inhabitants were wandering about over the country, like so many gypsies. In many instances, their beautiful homes, clustered around which were sacred ties and cherished memories of the past, were in ruins. Refugees were to be found everywhere. Many refined and cultured ladies had attached themselves to the army for protection, and served in any capacity where they could be of advantage to the cause.

While this deplorable state of affairs existed at the South it was far different at the North. They had

felt the effects of the war only in the loss of a few
from their home circles or of their friends. In fact,
the North was just getting in good shape to prolong
the war indefinitely. Her armies were well organized
and splendidly equipped. She had inexhaustible resources in men and money from which to draw.
Even Europe and Asia were her allies. Her people
at home were prosperous, being far removed from
the scene of bloody and devastating conflict. They
could pursue their daily avocations without molestation. Money was plentiful with them, and vast fortunes were accumulated in a short time. The war
was a great advantage to the North financially, and
many were the regrets, among a certain class of her
people, when it terminated, for it was impoverishing
the South and enriching the North. It was, nevertheless, true that some of our own people had im-
bibed, to a certain extent, the spirit of speculation
(and peculation) and had turned their attention to
profitable traffic. In some the allurements of gain
had completely absorbed their patriotic ardor, so conspicuous at the start.

Our gallant soldiers at the front, though they were
surrounded by so many depressing influences, never
failed to respond when duty called, even to baring
their breast to the deadly storm, or amid the roar of
battle to charge the enemy's breastworks.

CHAPTER XIV.

SUFFERING OF THE SOLDIERS—ATTACK ON TUN-
NEL HILL — ON MILL CREEK GAP—YANKS TRY
TO CATCH THE OLD WEASEL ASLEEP, BUT FAIL—
REPULSED AT DUG GAP—ALSO AT SNAKE CREEK
GAP—JOHNSTON EVACUATES DALTON AND OCCU-
PIES RESACCA—FIGHT AT RESACCA—AT FAR-
MERS FERRY—JOHNSTON AT CASSVILLE—NEW
HOPE CHURCH—KENNESAW—DEATH OF GENERAL
POLK — ATLANTA — JOHNSTON RELIEVED — SAD
FAREWELL.

For three months the army remained comparatively
inactive at Dalton. Several attempts to dislodge
Wheeler's cavalry at Tunnel Hill were made, but
without success. All were looking forward to a vigorous campaign to open in the spring. General Johnston was ever watchful of the movements of the
enemy while maturing his plans to meet their advance, which was sure to take place "when the buds
began to swell." The Confederate soldiers fared
badly during the winter at Dalton. Their sufferings
from cold and hunger were intense. Provisions were
of a very inferior quality and hard to obtain. Car-
loads of beeves were shipped from remote points in
the South, but owing to the delay in transportation
the cattle, when received, had become feverish and
much reduced in flesh, and many of them died on the
way; all, however, were issued to the soldiers. It
was that or nothing. The boys would take this
bloodshotten beef, put it into a camp kettle, throw in

a handful of salt, boil it awhile over the fire, take it out and wallow it over in the ashes; then, with a chunk of "hardtack," which could only be broken with a rock, sit down to appease their hunger. Thousands in that army, who had been accustomed to ease and luxury all their lives, were compelled to live on that character of diet during that fearful and stormy winter. Their clothing was inadequate to their comfort. Many of them were without blankets, shoes, or socks, and were compelled to go out in that pitiful plight to procure wood to keep them warm. General Johnston was doing everything in his power to remedy the evils and alleviate the sufferings of his soldiers. If the Federal General had been aware of the true condition of the Confederate army after the battle of Ringgold Gap, and had pushed on with his whole force, there is no doubt but that he would have crushed Bragg at Dalton.

I assert, without fear of successful contradiction, that General Pat Cleburne, by his heroic defense of Ringgold Gap, saved Bragg's army from annihilation.

By the time spring opened General Johnston had gotten his army in very good shape for defensive operations. The boys entered the field with renewed vigor and a determination to hurl death and destruction into the ranks of the invaders of their homes and firesides.

On, or about, the 23d of February, the Federals made a reconnoissance in force and attacked the Confederate cavalry at Tunnel Hill, the extreme outpost of the Confederates. After a brisk fight of over an hour the Confederates fell back from the town. They received reinforcements, turned upon the enemy, made a vigorous charge and retook the place. A determined attack was made, at the same time, on Mill Creek Gap, which was handsomely repulsed by Breckenridge's and Stewart's divisions. Several other points were attacked, but were easily held.

It seemed that these demonstrations were only made to feel the Confederate lines and determine their position, since there was no further movement made by the Federals until the first week in May, when a second attack, with a strong force of infantry, cavalry and artillery was made, which forced us to evacuate Tunnel Hill and fall back to the vicinity of Dalton.

This opened Sherman's world-wide "March to the Sea." He had at least 130,000 men, while the highest number Johnston had at any time to confront him with was 59,000, over two to one in favor of the Federals.

Their first attack was on Dug Gap. A desperate attempt was made to carry that point in order to strike Johnston's left flank. The Federals were met at the Gap by a brigade of Kentuckians under Colonel Wm. C. P. Breckenridge (and not by Grigsby, as some writers have stated). The Gap was held, and the enemy driven back in confusion, under the personal observation of General Hardee, who had been attracted to the spot by the heavy firing. He complimented the men and their commander for their heroic behavior at the time. Assaults were being made everywhere along the mountain slopes. The

Confederates, in every instance, held their ground and sent the enemy back discomfited.

Johnston had thrown down the gauntlet and invited Sherman to join issue with him in a general engagement, but the wily commander feared to take the risk, preferring to continue his flank movement, thinking, no doubt, that he might catch Johnston off his guard and strike an effectual blow at his rear. This scheme failed, however, for Johnston was "up to snuff," and was promptly advised as to the plans of his intrepid antagonist.

A determined attempt was made by McPherson, with twenty thousand men, to get possession of Resacca, by way of Snake Creek Gap, but it was handsomely repulsed.

It was then ascertained that the entire Federal army was moving in the direction of Snake Creek Gap. This forced Johnston to evacuate Dalton and occupy Resacca.

Sherman was figuring to effect a lodgment on the Western and Atlantic Railroad in Johnston's rear. A sharp fight occurred at Resacca, amounting almost to a battle, and, as usual, the Federals were repulsed.

Sherman continued his flank movement, which forced Johnston to give up Resacca and fall back to Tanner's Ferry. There the Federal advance was met and driven back by Hardee. They made a second advance, but were again repulsed by Hardee with heavy loss.

Johnston fell back to Adairsville, and from thence to Cassville. Fighting had become an every-day occupation. There was no cessation of hostilities from morning until night.

Sherman was a stirring fellow, and kept every moment of our time occupied.

At Cassville Johnston had determined, if possible, to bring on a general engagement, and had made all his arrangements with that end in view. Up to that time the fighting had only been done by detached portions of his army. He had his plans well laid and had the advantage as to position. The Federals came up in good style and opened a heavy artillery fire upon our lines. We thought, for a time, that the issue was to be decided then and there, but it was soon discovered that this was only a feint to cover a move in the direction of Marietta.

About this time Wheeler's cavalry captured a Federal wagon-train of over 200 wagons, loaded with supplies for Sherman's army. The men had been fasting for some time and were in fine condition to enjoy a feast. Canned fruits, vegetables and meats were found in profusion. It was a regular "hog-killing time" with the "boys." Johnston was forced to withdraw from Cassville, as Sherman was making a desperate effort to get in his rear. The corps of Hardee, Hood and Polk, were ordered at once to New Hope Church, where they met the enemy, and a battle was fought. The fight was desperate and bloody. Night only put a stop to the carnage. The Federals were badly crippled. Many of them took refuge in a ravine close by, under cover of the night. During the night it was found out that some of the enemy were still in their place of concealment, and the Confederates charged the position, drove them out, captured over 300 prisoners and 1,200 stands of arms. The Federals *acknowledged* a loss, in that engagement, of over 1,500 men. The Confederate loss was about 80 men killed and 300 wounded. The next day the fight was renewed on another part of the line, and the Confederates were repulsed with a loss of several hundred men.

After the operations just related, Johnston, discovering that Sherman was still forging his way along his flank, withdrew from Allatoona and Acworth and took up a new position near Kennesaw Mountain.

General Sherman took possession of Allatoona, where there is a deep cut through which the railroad passes. He fortified the place and left a garrison of 800 men to protect it. An effort was made by the Confederates to capture this stronghold, but after several attempts, they were repulsed with great loss and were forced to retire.

While all this fighting was going on, our cavalry was actively employed doing all the damage possible to Sherman's transportation along the line of the Western and Atlantic railroad. The cavalry were provided with ten tubes an inch in diameter, and from a foot to eighteen inches in length. These tubes were filled with powder and the ends closed. Whenever they could obtain access to a woodpile beside the track they would bore holes in the ends of the sticks, insert a tube, plug up the holes, replace the stick, retire and await results. These operations were carried on during the night. We knew of a number of explosions taking place on the engines but never heard of any very serious accidents occurring from the experiment.

The W. & A. railroad was the great lever power which enabled Sherman and his army to penetrate to the heart of the Confederacy. Without it he could never have accomplished his object. Sherman was too good a general to venture so far from his base of supplies without direct communication by rail. Sherman's force was sufficient to keep Johnston moving back, and at the same time furnish a heavy guard for the protection of all important points along the line. He had the plan of every bridge along the line and whenever our men would destroy any one of them, he would have it duplicated without delay.

Everything looked like a great battle was near at hand. The lines were drawing close together for that purpose.

Just here a calamity occurred which spread a mantle of gloom over the Confederate army. General Polk, with several other officers, rode to the top of Kennesaw mountain to view the situation, when a shell from one of the enemy's batteries exploded in their midst, killing General Polk almost instantly. The writer was within a few feet of him when he fell.

The position of the confederate forces along the base and extending to the crest of Kennesaw Mountain, was a splendid one and overlooked the country in all directions, which rendered it impossible for Sherman to conceal his movements. The Confederate batteries were along the top of the mountain at different points, and the fire from their guns at night upon the Federal lines in the valley below presented

a wild and lurid appearance. The screaming shells
as they went circling through the midnight gloom,
looked like fiery demons on their passage to the in-
fernal regions. It was a sight never to be forgotten
by those who witnessed it.

The Federals continued to press onward while Johnson's little army calmly awaited their coming; having
such entire confidence in the skill and strategic genius
of their commander, they had no fear of the result.

The details of the battle will not be attempted in
these sketches. Suffice it to say, that the Confederates
held their lines at every point of attack and hurled
the enemy back with fearful loss. It was one of the
fiercest struggles of the war.

Sherman saw that he could not dislodge Johnston
from his almost impregnable position without haz—
arding the loss of his army, so he resorted to his old
tactics of a "flank movement." This forced Johnston
to fall back to the Chattahoochee, which he crossed
and burned the bridge after him. This threw Johnston in close proximity to Atlanta, which was envi-
roned by a network of redoubts and rifle-pits.

Sherman replaced the immense bridge across the
Chattahoochee in so short a time that he was ever
afterwards regarded by our boys as the champion
bridge-builder of the world.

Fighting was continued to the very gates of the
doomed city. The boys then took to the trenches as
ducks to water. There they could have defended the
city indefinitely had it not been for an unexpected
order, which came like an electric bolt from a clear
sky and shattered all their hopes. This was an order

from the authorities at Richmond, relieving General Johnston from the command and naming General John B. Hood to succeed him. That order sent Sherman rejoicing on his way to the sea and the Confederacy to her grave.

This noble army of heroic Confederates, blood-stained from a hundred battle-fields, had received a stab from which they could never recover. They had lost their beloved commander. It was the worst blow ever dealt to the army of Tennessee. It was a mortal wound, a death-blow to the Confederacy. Sherman himself, could not have suggested a move that would have been more to his advantage.

Johnston had successfully conducted the most masterly retrograde movement of modern times. For two months he had held an army in check which outnumbered his own more than two to one. He had inflicted heavy losses upon the enemy at every move he had made. Johnston's army, on reaching Atlanta, was in much better condition to confront Sherman than when the campaign opened at Dalton, two months before. The *esprit de corps* of Johnston's army was unsurpassed by that of Napoleon's grand army. With one stroke of the pen a fatal step had been taken, which was fraught with greater disaster to that heroic army than Sherman, with his 160,000 men had been able to inflict. Far better would it have been to have disbanded that army and turned the country over to the Yankees than to have changed commanders at this inopportune moment. Thousands of lives which were sacrificed to no purpose would

9 b g

have been saved. Such a stroke of policy as changing commanders right in the face of the enemy when all previous plans must be changed, has not a parallel in the annals of war.

Hood realized the great mistake, but brave, gallant and dashing soldier that he was, he could but accept the inevitable.

It was a sad scene when those smoke-begrimed and battle-scarred veterans gathered around their beloved chief to bid him a final good-bye! Not a word was spoken, but with quivering lips and eyes bedimmed with tears, they grasped his hand and turned in silence from the scene. The general himself was too full to speak ; he could only respond in a faltering voice to their warm and friendly grasps: " Go do your duty."

It might not have affected the final result, but it scarcely admits of a doubt that Sherman would never have reached the sea with his army intact had Johnston remained in command.

CHAPTER XV.

HOOD TAKES THE OFFENSIVE—ATTACKS SHER-
MAN—IS REPULSED—PANDEMONIUM REIGNS IN
ATLANTA—BATTLE OF JULY 22D—RAID ON MA-
CON—STONEMAN CAPTURED—A REGIMENT ES-
CAPES — THEIR CAPTURE—ATHENS — A GRAND
OVATION—A RAGGED PRIVATE OUR ORATOR.

Hood was a dashing officer and a hard fighter.
After the removal of Johnston, the entire program of
the campaign was changed. Sherman, for the time,
suspended offensive movements and took up a strong
position on Peachtree creek, north of Atlanta. He,
no doubt, expected to draw Hood into a general engagement there. Hood accepted the challenge and
made an impetuous assault upon the Federal army,
but was repulsed with heavy loss. Our army fell
back to Atlanta under a heavy fire from the enemy's
batteries, located to the left of the Peachtree road.

We found the city in a wild state of excitement.
Citizens were running in every direction. Terror-
stricken women and children went screaming about
the streets seeking some avenue of escape from hiss-
ing, bursting shells, as they sped on their mission of
death and destruction. Perfect pandemonium reigned
near the union depot. Trunks, bedclothing and
wearing apparel were scattered in every direction.
People were striving in every conceivable way to get
out of town with their effects.

In the meantime, Sherman was moving on like a
besom of destruction, scattering fire in every direction.

A heavy battle took place between Atlanta and Decatur on the 22d of July. This checked Sherman's advance for the moment, but the Gate City of the South was doomed. The Confederates held their ground, but they gained no advantage.

In this battle of the 22d the Federals lost one of their favorite officers, General McPherson. The Confederate general, W. H. T. Walker, was also killed. Both armies sustained heavy loss in killed and wounded.

It was ascertained that the Federal general, Stoneman, had started, with a heavy column of cavalry, in the direction of Macon. It was thought that his objective point was Andersonville, where a large number of Federal prisoners of war were confined. A force of Confederate cavalry under General Iverson, was ordered in pursuit.

General Johnston, on his retirement from the army at Atlanta, repaired to Macon, at that time a depot of supplies for the Confederate army.

Shortly after Johnston reached Macon he found out that a large Federal cavalry force was moving in the direction of that place, and at once collected the attaches of the various departments located there, formed them into a small army and moved out to intercept Stoneman on his approach to the town.

The Federal commander, finding that he was confronted by a force, and heavily pressed in his rear, decided that the best policy for him to pursue was to surrender, and sent a flag of truce into our lines. The terms upon which General Iverson received the surrender were unconditional. While taking account of the men and arms, one of the Federal colonels, with about 300 men, slipped off, with a view of making their way back to the Federal lines. When this was ascertained a detachment of Confederate cavalry was sent in pursuit.

We came up with their rear guard just about daybreak, near a little place called "Jug Tavern." We charged the column, captured the party and carried the prisoners to Athens, as that was the nearest point from which we could get transportation by rail for them. As the town of Athens was somewhat isolated and situated some distance from the principal thoroughfares, her people had, up to that time, felt very slightly the effects of the war. They never had seen a Yankee soldier and but very few Confederates. The whole population was thrown into a state of excitement when we marched our prisoners into town and placed them inside the college campus with a guard around them.

Our men and horses were very nearly exhausted from long and heavy marches, hunger and lack of sleep. Notwithstanding all this, we were heroes, the observed of all observers. The people of the "Classic City" treated us with enthusiastic consideration. They supplied us with plenty of good things to eat and gave us an ovation in the college chapel. The large auditorium was crowded to its utmost capacity with the youth and beauty of Athens.

No city in the South surpasses Athens in the culture and refinement of its inhabitants. Its educational facilities are unsurpassed. Hundreds of wealthy families from different sections of the South have made Athens their home on account of its health-giving influences and the splendid advantages it offers for the education of their sons and daughters.

On the occasion referred to, the back part of the auditorium was occupied by the soldiers, while the front was given up to the ladies. On the rostrum were seated the mayor and a few distinguished gentlemen, either too old to be in the army, or, by their professions, exempted. Our soldiers were a motley looking set compared with those well-dressed people. We had not seen our wagon-train for a month and were as dirty as pigs !

The exercises were opened with prayer, which was followed by an eloquent speech by the mayor of the city. He paid glowing tributes to the soldiers and eulogized their deeds of daring in a chaste and elegant manner. When he concluded, it became necessary for some soldier to reply. First one was called upon, then another, but all seemed backward in facing that audience in their pitiable plight. Finally, one of the boys, a private, was pushed out into the aisle and almost forced forward. He was a private soldier, nineteen or twenty years of age. (I mention this to give some idea what kind of material composed the rank and file of our army.) With a great deal of hesitation he managed to reach the platform. All eyes were turned with astonishment upon this smoke-begrimed soldier-boy, and all seemed amazed to think he should be put forward to reply to the elegant address of their mayor. The comments we overheard were by no means flattering. Several elegantly dressed ladies occupied the seat just in front of the writer, who, overhearing some of their comments on

the ludicrous appearance of our soldier-boy, remarked
to them that, if they would withhold their criticisms
for a moment, they might find themselves mistaken.
To make the matter worse, our soldier wore a gray
jacket which fell far short of concealing two very
large abrasions in the seat of his pants, caused by long
contact with the saddle. His attempt on the stage
to stretch his jacket in order to hide this defect,
brought forth a shout from all parts of the house.
He was indeed an object of pity rather than of mirth.
His hair was in a tangled mass, and his shirt had not
felt the cleansing influence of water for months.
With all these visible defects, the young man braced
himself for the conflict, and with one sweeping glance
over the sea of faces, he addressed himself to the
"chair" with an ease and grace of manner which
showed he was no novice in the part he was called
upon to perform. As he warmed up to his subject,
everyone seemed to loose sight of his outward appearance. His lofty and sublime thoughts, clothed in
classically chosen language and expressed with that
impassioned eloquence which always commands attention and respect, completely captivated his hearers.
The excitement of the crowd at times, when he would
round off a beautiful period, became intense, and
would only subside after a wild burst of applause.
When he told, in gentle cadence, of his home within
the enemy's lines, over a thousand miles away, and
how he parted with his mother and sister and bade
his classmates in college adieu, to take up arms for
the struggling South, and of the hardships he had
endured, there was scarcely a dry eye in the house.

He held the crowd spellbound for an hour. When he descended from the rostrum the ladies gathered about him, anxious to grasp the hand of the soldier orator and congratulate him on his magnificent effort. Never before, nor since, has that old hall resounded with such burning eloquence!

Many who read this will recognize the subject of the sketch, when I tell them that the young man who made that speech stands high in the councils of the nation, and is acknowledged to-day as one of the most gifted orators of the South. His name and fame extend far beyond the limits of his native State. After the war he studied law in one of the principal cities of the South, was soon admitted to the bar, and in a very short time took his stand in the front rank of his profession. His brilliant career has been watched with pride and admiration by his many warm and devoted friends and comrades scattered all over this broad Southland. He is one of Georgia's representatives in the United States Congress.

CHAPTER XVI.

HOOD'S COUNTERMARCH—TURNS HIS BACK ON
SHERMAN AND MOVES ON TENNESSEE—SHER-
MAN'S DESOLATING MARCH—IN SAVANNAH—HOW
WE SUBSISTED—WHEELER'S LAST ORDER—DE-
FENSE OF THE CONFEDERATE CAVALRY—HOOD'S
DISASTERS.

It was evident on our return to the army that the
change of commanders was fraught with many disasters. The battles fought in and around Atlanta
gained no advantage to the Confederacy.

Hood, of his own volition, or prompted by orders
from Richmond, changed the program of the campaign, and, to the utter dismay of every one of us,
reversed his position and faced his army in the direction of Tennessee, marching it over a territory that
had been swept clean by two contending armies.
This move left Sherman's army clear to march, un-
obstructed, to the sea.

It is stated on good authority that when Sherman
became aware of Hood's plans he offered to furnish
him rations to go with, so well pleased was he with
the change, knowing that it would be impossible for
him to continue his march with Hood's army in his
front.

The death-knell of the Confederacy had been
sounded; Atlanta had gone up in smoke, and nothing
remained to prevent Sherman, with sword and torch,
from laying waste the fair homes and fertile fields of
Georgia and the Carolinas, a small force of cavalry

being all that was left to impede his march of destruction to the coast.   The daily skirmishing with
his advance guard had no more effect than a fly would
have on the back of a sea turtle.

Sherman moved on without any interruption, leaving a black and smoldering trail of ruin behind him.
Thousands of negroes, with their plunder, flocked to
the Federal army as it passed through the country.
When the crowd became too burdensome the Federals would take up their bridges at the crossing of
some river and leave their poor, deluded followers on
the opposite bank, to ponder over the mutability of
human plans and to cast a longing look at the re-
ceding forms of their supposed deliverers.

Sherman finally reached Savannah and captured
that beautiful "City by the Sea" without a struggle.

The Confederacy had played its last card and was
tottering on the verge of a collapse.

While Sherman's army was feasting in Savannah
on the luxuries of the land and sea the Confederates
were wallowing about in the swamps adjacent to the
city subsisting on what could be gleaned from the
abandoned rice fields, with now and then a turtle and
a few small fish thrown in.   This dish, cooked without any salt, would be extremely revolting to any one
but a Confederate soldier.   This was about the extent of our diet for a month, while Sherman was in
Savannah.

It was about this time that General Wheeler issued
his last order to his troops.   The following is an exact copy :

" HEADQUARTERS CAVALRY CORPS,
" December 31st, 1864.

" MY BRAVE SOLDIERS :—The close of this year
terminates a campaign of eight months, during which
you have been engaged in continuous and successful
fighting. From Dalton to Atlanta, you held the
right of our army, opposed continuously by a force
of infantry ten times your number. You repulsed
every assault, inflicting upon the enemy a loss, in
killed and wounded, numerically greater than your
entire strength. Every attempt on the part of the
enemy to turn or strike our right flank was met and
repulsed by your determined valor and courage. It
should be a proud reflection to you all, that during
the entire campaign the Army of Tennessee never
lost a position by having the flank which it was your
duty to protect, turned. During every movement of
our lines you have been between our infantry and the
enemy, hurling back his exulting advance, and holding the entire army at bay until our troops had quietly
prepared to receive and repulse his gigantic assault.

" Having failed by other means to drive our army
from their position in front of Atlanta, he now sends
three heavy columns of cavalry to destroy our communications, to release prisoners of war, and march
in triumph with them through the country. You
promptly struck one column and drove it back discomfited, then quickly assaulted the two others, defeated them and completed their capture. This alone
cost the enemy more than five thousand men, horses
and arms, besides material, colors and cannon. This
was due to your valor, and is without parallel in the
history of this war. Having been detached and sent
to the rear of the enemy you captured his garrisons,
destroyed his stores, and broke his communications
more effectually and for longer than any force, however large, has done.

"During Sherman's march through Georgia you retarded his advance and defeated his cavalry daily, preventing his spreading over and devastating the whole country. During the last five months you have traveled nearly three thousand miles, fighting nearly every day, and always with success. You have been victorious in more than fifty pitched battles and a hundred minor affairs, placing the enemy ' hors de combat' fully four times the greatest number you ever carried into battle.

" I desire, my brave soldiers, to thank you for your gallantry, devotion and good conduct. Every position I have asked you to hold has been held until absolutely untenable. Your devotion to your country fills my heart with gratitude. You have done your full duty to your country and to me, and I have tried to do my full duty to you. Circumstances have forced upon you many and great deprivations. You have been deprived of the issue of clothing and many of the comforts and conveniences which other troops have enjoyed. You have borne all without a murmur.

" Soldiers of Kentucky, Tennessee, Texas and Arkansas, you deserve commendation for your sacrifices and fortitude. Separated from your homes and families, you have nobly done all that gallant, devoted men could do.

" Soldiers of Alabama and Georgia, your homes have nearly all been overrun and destroyed. Yet, without complaint you have stood at your colors like brave and patriotic men. Your country and your God will one day reward you. The gallant Kelly, whom we all loved so well, is dead. Many other brave men, whose loss we deeply feel, sleep with him. They fell, the price of victory. Allen, Humes, Anderson, Hogan, Ashly, Harrison, Breckenridge and many other brave men, whose gallantry you so often

have witnessed, are here still, to guide and lead you
in battles yet to be fought with the same valor I have
always seen you exhibit upon the many fields where
your determined courage has won victory for your
cause.

"J. WHEELER,
"Major-General."

The writer quotes the above order, to show in
what high estimation the Commanding General held
that important arm of the service. General Wheeler
was an accomplished officer. He graduated with distinguished honor at the United States Military Academy at West Point, just as the war commenced.
With an experience of four years' active service
in the field, at the head of a large cavalry force, he
was well calculated to judge as to its efficiency.

Notwithstanding the harsh criticisms at times hurled
at the cavalry, there was no branch of the Confederate army that fought more battles, suffered greater
privations, endured more hardships, or were brought
face to face in more hand-to-hand engagements with
the enemy. The other arms of the service had their
periods of rest and recuperation ; the cavalrymen were
constantly on the move; their home was in the saddle. Ever vigilant and watchful, they must report
with accuracy every movement of the enemy. They
were frequently sent over mountains, hills and glens,.
on long marches to the enemy's rear, to strike a blow
at some point on their line of communication. No
kind of weather retarded these movements. They
often marched all night in a drenching rain, and
when permitted to halt for a few hours' rest, were·

compelled to do so with their blankets and clothes saturated with water.

The reason so many slurs were cast at the cavalry, was because they were compelled to draw largely upon the country through which they passed for subsistence. Their clothing, horses and equipments, as a general thing, were captured from the enemy. The blue overcoats worn by the Federals they found to be very comfortable. Sometimes they captured large quantities of them at the principal depots of supplies. In order to utilize these garments it became necessary to change their color. Without which they were liable to be mistaken by our own men for the enemy. The process of changing the color of these uniforms was accomplished in this manner: "A large washpot was furnished by some kind lady in the neighborhood; the pot was filled with water, into which was placed a quantity of bark from the walnut-tree with a little copperas to set the color." This is why the Yankees applied the appellation of "Butternut Rangers" to our cavalry.

It would require many volumes to present the many marvelous and daring exploits of the Confederate cavalry. No mention has ever been made of hundreds of engagements in which they were engaged, which would have been considered as fierce battles in other wars. These are only remembered by those who participated in them. The bones of hundreds of these brave cavalrymen lie scattered along the entire line, from the banks of the Rio Grande to the Ohio. The mountains and valleys of Mississippi, Kentucky, Tennessee, Virginia, the Carolinas and Georgia were crimsoned with their blood. The cold pages of history must ever remain as mute as the hills and valleys on which they fought as to their many acts of individual heroism. No head-stone marks the spot where many of these brave soldiers fell. They belong to the great army of the "Unknown." The wild winds must chant their requiem, and no loving hands will strow their lone graves with nature's choicest gems.

"Underneath the dewy grasses,
Pale and silently they sleep!
Waiting for God's sounding bugle,
While the flowers their vigils keep."

Hood's campaign into Tennessee resulted almost in the annihilation of his entire army. He hurled his columns against strongly fortified positions, where they were swept away by the deadly fire of the enemy, in superior numbers, behind almost impregnable breastworks.

It was on the bloody heights of Franklin that the immortal Cleburn fell, with his dead and dying comrades all around him! The loss of such an officer was almost irreparable. The noble soldier's desire was gratified, however, for he had often been heard to say: "I had rather fall in battle than live to see the cause I have fought for go down in defeat."

After the terrible disasters he sustained in front of Franklin and Nashville, Hood had no alternative but to retrace his steps with the pitiable fragment of an army which had held in check for two months Sherman's combined forces, outnumbering them over two to one. These movements have no parallel in history.

The writer will not attempt in these sketches to locate the responsibility of Hood's unfortunate march into Tennessee. That must be left for the historian who has laboriously studied the record of "The War of the Rebellion" to determine. It was the general impression at that time that that grand army was sacrificed on the altar of prejudice and malice.

CHAPTER XVII.

SHERMAN'S PROPOSAL TO HILL—LINCOLN AND THE
COMMISSIONERS—SHERMAN BEGINS HIS MARCH
FROM SAVANNAH—OUR COOK'S IDEA OF HONG-
KONG GOOSE AND RICE.

While the Confederacy was gasping for breath, and
defeat was staring her in the face, some overtures
were being made for peace. One of these should not
be overlooked, as it furnishes an historic incident of
the great civil war never before given to the public.
It is a scrap of unwritten history, of which we should
not lose sight, as it shows there was a disposition on
the part of a distinguished officer in the Federal army
to stop the useless effusion of blood and destruction of
property. It occurred while Sherman occupied Atlanta.

The late Hon. Joshua Hill, a prominent Union man
who took strong grounds against secession, had a son
in the Confederate army who was killed at the battle
of Kennesaw Mountain. Colonel Hill visited Atlanta to obtain a permit from General Sherman to remove the remains of his son to his home in Madison,
Ga., for interment. General Sherman received
Colonel Hill very cordially and furnished him with
the necessary passport which enabled him to secure
the object so much desired.

Colonel Hill related to Dr. John F. Patterson, a
warm, personal friend of his, the substance of his
interview with Sherman. Dr. Patterson is the only

living witness, at this late day, to whom the statement was made, and from whom it was obtained by the writer; all other parties mentioned in connection with this visit of Colonel Hill's to Atlanta have passed to their long home.

Colonel Hill stated to his friend, Dr. Patterson, that his interview with General Sherman was very pleasant and lasted most of the night. The conversation was principally confined to the war. Sherman asked Hill if there was no chance for a speedy termination of the war; and expressed a desire, on his part, that the struggle should end. He told Colonel Hill that, if Governor Brown would assume the responsibility over the State of Georgia and stop all hostilities in the State, he would discontinue his march to the sea, and would not destroy another dollar's worth of property in the State. It was agreed that Colonel Hill should seek Governor Brown at once and make known to him the proposition, and, at the same time, to use his influence in the matter. Governor Brown had gone to Augusta with the archives of the State, to which point Hill repaired without delay. He communicated to Governor Brown Sherman's proposition. After a lengthy discussion, in which several distinguished gentlemen participated, Governor Brown declined to accede. While he considered it fair and honorable, he said, or rather intimated, that, owing to the feverish condition of the people, he thought that to accept the terms, just at that time, would not be wise, on the ground that it would endanger *his own safety.* Colonel Hill's mission was at an end. He returned to

Sherman and reported the result. Sherman remarked: "There is nothing left for me to do but to proceed."

The above statement can be relied upon as *authentic*. It came from one of Georgia's most distinguished sons. It made such impression on Dr. Patterson that he made a note of it at the time.

Colonel Hill had twice represented his district in the National Congress, and was sent to the United States Senate at the close of the war. He was largely instrumental in bringing about the harmony and good feeling between the two sections, and bringing peace and quiet to his distracted country. The South owes Colonel Hill a debt of gratitude she can never repay for his distinguished services in her behalf at that critical period.

In connection with the above proposition prominent gentlemen from the North had visited Richmond with a view to bringing the war to a close. They had, in consequence of a strong feeling at the North in favor of peace, constituted themselves mediators between the two sections. Their object was to bring about an armistice, that the matter might be talked over by officials from both sides. The result of the visit to the capital of the Confederate States brought about what was known as the "Hampton Roads Conference."

The eminent gentlemen selected by Mr. Davis to represent the Confederacy at this conference were Hon. Alexander H. Stephens, Hon. R. M. T. Hunter and Hon. John A. Campbell—all men of national reputation. These gentlemen, by previous agree-

ment, passed through the Federal lines, and from
thence to Fortress Monroe. The interview took
place on board a steamer, which lay at anchor near
the fort. Mr. Lincoln and Mr. Seward represented
the United States Government.

All eyes were centered upon the result of this
conference, for there was not a soldier in the ranks
of the Confederate army but knew and felt that any
further effort by force of arms to establish their independence would be utterly useless.

The South was conquered and within the grasp
of three mighty armies—Grant on one side, Sherman on the other, and Thomas in the rear. The
South had done all that it was possible for human
skill and ingenuity to accomplish with her resources; there was no alternative but to submit to
the arbitrament of the sword which was against us.

The terms offered by Mr. Lincoln were better than
we had any reason to expect. Mr. Lincoln gave
the commissioners from the South to understand that
he could enter into no negotiations with them as
commissioners from the Confederate States, but that
he was ready and willing to treat with them on the
reconstruction of the Union. He further stated,
which is part of the official record, that if resistance
would cease, and the national authority was recognized, the seceded States would be immediately
restored to their practical relations to the Union.
He went on further to say that he believed the people of the North would be willing to be taxed to the
extent of remunerating the South for the loss of their
slaves, if the war would cease without further expense

and bloodshed. Our commissioners, not being clothed with discretionary powers, could not act upon this most favorable and generous proposition. They were instructed to negotiate upon no other terms than the unconditional recognition of the Confederate States.

This was preposterous in the extreme, when it is considered that the Federal armies held possession of almost the entire country. It reminded one of the "evil spirit" when he took our Savior up into an exceeding high mountain and offered him all the kingdoms of the world if he would but fall down and worship him; at the same time the poor devil had no claim to a foot of land on the earth.

After our commissioners learned the ultimatum of Mr. Lincoln, they had no alternative but to return to Richmond without having accomplished anything. Mr. Stephens was so depressed at the result of the conference that he at once withdrew from Richmond to his home in Crawfordville, there to abide the result, whatever it might be; no doubt with the one comforting solace—

"Let Fate do her worst, there are relics of joy,
Bright dreams of the past, she cannot destroy."

History furnishes no parallel to the case in point, where the vanquished attempted to dictate terms to the victor. There is no doubt but had the whole matter been left to the three envoys from the South, such terms could have been agreed upon as would have relieved the people in the Southern States from the great humiliation incident to reconstruction,

through which they were compelled ultimately to
pass. Where the blame should rest let the future
chronicler of those events determine. We know
this much : a look of blank despair settled upon all,
when the result of the conference became known.

It was evident to every one that Mr. Lincoln
never would have left Washington and gone to
Fortress Monroe unless he had expected to make a
liberal and generous proposition for peace. Mr.
Stephens stated, some time after the war closed, that
the terms were far better than we had any reason,
under the circumstances, to expect. To say the least,
it was a fatal mistake. The soldiers on both sides
were tired of the strife. Those in the Southern army
were willing to press on if they could see a possible
chance of success.

Sherman, after resting his army for a month,
moved out of Savannah and continued his march
through the Carolinas.

I was evident that he contemplated forming a
junction with Grant somewhere in Virginia ; then
wind up the ball in short order.

Now our old duties, skirmishing with Sherman's
advance, commenced again. These skirmishes frequently resulted in sharp and bloody engagements.
Anything was preferable to the hum-drum of camp
life in south Georgia (the " low-grounds of sorrow,"
as we boys called it), where we were compelled to
subsist on Hong-Kong geese and boiled rice.

Quite an amusing incident occurred with one of
our up-country darkies while preparing one of our
savory meals. The negro, who had always prided

himself on his culinary skill, parboiled his ancient and venerable fowl, for a few hours, in a large camp-kettle, then added about a peck of rice. He was not long in discovering that something was wrong and called to one of the soldiers standing near by to step there a moment. With his eyes protruding and his mouth stretched from ear to ear, he thus expostulated:

"Bless de Lord, marster, I jest put in one of dem buckets full of dat ar stuff wid de goose, an' ef I ain't dipped out enough to ration de whole Yankee army, I ain't no nigger, sho'; an' she's still a-comin'!"

CHAPTER XVIII.

SHERMAN'S DEVASTATING MARCH—RUIN IN SOUTH
CAROLINA — COLUMBIA EVACUATED — THE
WOUNDED TENNESSEEAN—LADIES IN DISTRESS—
HOW I AIDED THEM—COLUMBIA A MUNDANE
HELL—A NIGHT OF HORRORS—MY FEDERAL
FRIEND CARES FOR MY LADY FRIEND AND THE
WOUNDED SOLDIER.

The small force in Sherman's front offered but
slight resistance to his advance. He swept on with
his army of sixty thousand men, like a full developed
cyclone, leaving behind him a track of desolation
and ashes fifty miles wide. In front of them was
terror and dismay. Bummers and foragers swarmed
on his flanks, who plundered and robbed every one
who was so unfortunate as to be within their reach.

It seemed that the Federals were inspired with
renewed hatred and malice when they struck the soil
of South Carolina. Poor, bleeding, suffering South
Carolina! Up to that time she had felt but slightly
(away from the coast) the devastating effects of the
war; but her time had come. The protestations of
her old men and the pleadings of her noble women
had no effect in staying the ravages of sword, flame
and pillage.

Columbia's fate could readily be foretold from the
destruction along Sherman's line of march after he
left Savannah. Beautiful homes, with their tropical
gardens, which had been the pride of their owners
for generations, were left in ruins and the inhabitants

turned out to starve. Everything that could not be carried off, was destroyed. Thousands who had but recently lived in affluence were compelled to subsist on the scrapings from the abandoned camps of the soldiers. The negroes were in nowise exempt. They suffered in proportion with the whites. Live stock of every description, that they could not make use of, was shot down. All farm implements, with wagons and vehicles of every description, were given to the flames.

The last stand made by our troops, before reaching Columbia, was at the covered bridge over Broad river, where a desperate fight took place, but it was all to no purpose. The bridge was burned, and we fell back in the direction of Columbia.

Hasty preparations were being made to evacuate the place. General Beauregard, with a small force, occupied the city. He succeeded in removing most of the government supplies.

When the last of the stores had been sent out, the writer, with a detachment of cavalry, was ordered to remain and clear the city of stragglers, and to remove all sick and wounded soldiers from the hospitals who were able to travel. While on this duty I found in one of the wards a young soldier-boy from Tennessee, who was suffering from a wound in the hip. He was a bright, intelligent young fellow. He was not able to be moved a long distance, but plead manfully to be taken along, as he could not bear the thought of falling into the hands of the Yankees; besides, he was weary and tired out with hospital life

and desired a change.   I told him that I would see
what could be done for him.

While passing along one of the streets I was ac-
costed by a well-dressed lady, apparently in great
distress.   She asked if I thought the city would be
destroyed.   I told her that I did not think there was
any doubt about it.   This information seemed to distress her very much.   She informed me that she had
an invalid mother at home and was fearful that the
shock might prove fatal to her.   She pleadingly
asked if I would not step down to the house with
her, as it was but a short distance from where we
were standing, and I might be able to make some
suggestion to their advantage.

I accompanied the young lady to her spacious residence, located in the center of a square of beautiful
magnolias.   The house was elegantly furnished, and
I saw at a glance that all the appointments indicated
its occupants were people of wealth and refinement.
I was informed by the lady that there were no gentlemen connected with the household at that time ;
that she had two brothers but they were both in the
army of Virginia ; that her mother was a widow, and
her brothers had not been at home in eighteen
months.   They had some very trusty servants, but
they would not do to rely upon at such times, for
there was an element in the Federal army (by no
means American) who would subject these poor
ignorant creatures to the most cruel and inhuman
tortures, that they might extort from them the
hiding places of valuables.

I became interested in the family and decided to

make an effort to protect them if possible. I remarked to the young lady, who, judging from her appearance, was not long out of her teens, that I would see what could be done for them; that all would depend upon my communicating with a friend, who was an officer in the Federal army, and this must be done before they took possession of the city. I had learned from prisoners captured at different times that my friend was in Sherman's army, and serving on the staff of one of his general officers. It might be well enough to state in this connection, that the friend alluded to was the Federal officer who figured in a little episode on the Rio Grande at the breaking out of the war, the same whose exchange I assisted in effecting when the armies were in Tennessee. I stated to the young lady that in order to carry out the program I had mapped out, it would be necessary for her to act in the capacity of nurse for a short while; that I had a young friend in one of the hospitals of the city suffering from a painful wound—a bright, intelligent young man from one of the first families of Tennessee, and that if she would provide a room for him and act as his nurse, it would greatly facilitate my purpose; to which proposition she readily assented. I at once dispatched two soldiers who were with me, to lose no time in procuring an ambulance and removing the wounded soldier to the new quarters I had secured for him. I remained to complete details, as we had no time to lose. I suggested that perhaps it would be well for her to collect, with the assistance of some of her lady friends, all or the most of their valuables, and place them in as secure a place as she could find,

but to be sure to have no negroes present, however
reliable or trusty she might think them. I then informed the young lady that the mayor, with some
other officials of Columbia, were then contemplating
going out to surrender the city, that if she would
furnish me with writing materials I would address a
communication to my friend, and, through the may-
or's party, try to get it inside the Federal lines. I
stated in my letter the circumstances of the wounded
soldier and the family where he was located, and told
my friend that if it was within his power and consist-
ent with his public duties, he would confer a very
great favor upon me by giving them protection, and
gave him the address of the young lady. Just as I
had finished writing, the ambulance drove up with
the young man. We were not long in transferring
him to comfortable apartments, and turning him over
to the tender care of the fair young hostess. He expressed himself as delighted with the change. I informed the young lady that if the officer should call,
she would have no reason to regret it, for she would
find him a cultured and polished gentleman, one of
the true Southern stripe; a Kentuckian and could be
trusted.

I left immediately to confer with the mayor and
his party, but told her that I would soon return. I
found the mayor's party just on the eve of starting on
their mission. Among the number was one of the
prominent ministers of the city, to whom I related
the circumstances, and he very kindly promised to
use his best efforts to have the message reach its des-
tination.

We soon got everything in shape to move. I directed the command to proceed to a point about a mile north of the city and there remain until I came up.

I took three soldiers with me and returned to the house of the young lady for the purpose of giving some further instructions. We found the place in confusion. Other ladies had been added to the number, and acting upon their young hostess's suggestion, were seeking a safe place for their valuables. They seemed to be fearful that all would be lost in spite of the efforts that had been made. I offered them a word of encouragement by stating that if my communication reached the hands of the officer to whom it had been addressed, before the army took possession of the city, they need have no apprehension that their interests would not be looked after, and without some unavoidable accident, their persons and property would be protected.

It was quite natural that I should be anxious to know the result of my efforts in behalf of these fair Southern ladies, as soon as possible. In order to procure the much-desired information at the very earliest possible moment, I had conferred with a brave and gallant soldier, one who could be relied on in any emergency (at this late date he is a prosperous business man in one of our Southern cities, where he has been frequently called upon by his fellow citizens to fill important positions of trust and honor). I explained to the young lady the plan agreed upon by the soldier and myself, which was as follows: He was to retire to some secluded place

outside the city, and there remain concealed, until
after dark ; then make his way into the city, and, if
they had not been disturbed, seek to communicate
with the lady. The plan agreed upon was, if the
house was under guard, for him to approach from
the rear side, under cover of a hedge of arborvitæ ;
and for her to take a seat near a window, which must
be slightly raised (no light to be in the room), and,
at a given signal, slip out of the window a paper,
which she must have already prepared, giving a brief
statement of how our plans had succeeded.   This
was in order to avoid any verbal communication with
the soldier. She was a brave girl and readily acceded to the plans. The soldier understood his duty,
for he had been on dangerous missions before.

All arrangements being completed, we bade the
young lady good-bye and took our departure. I desire to state that the three soldiers mentioned and
myself were the last of the Confederates to leave
Columbia on that stormy and eventful day.

Not a vestige of fire was visible in any part of the
city when we went out.   This, I trust, may be
another link in the chain of evidence that goes to
prove that the Confederates were, in no way, connected with the burning of that fair city of the
South ; a belief which was held for a long time by
many people of the North, but which has since been
refuted by the very best and most reliable authority.
It was Sherman's army that burned Columbia; not
the Confederates.   Whether he was personally responsible for it or not, I am not prepared to say, but
Sherman was in command, and he was a disciplina-

rian. This much I do know, that, while Sherman's advance came in on one side of the city, we retired on the opposite. We repaired to an elevation about a mile to the north of the city, and, from that commanding spot, witnessed the terrible conflagration which destroyed that proud and heroic city of the South. It was from this point that we saw the flames burst forth from public buildings, stores, and beautiful homesteads, including that of General Hampton, which had long been the pride of a refined and cultured people.

Columbia was in flames. Then it was that the demons of fire commenced their exploits of rapine and pillage. Stores and dwellings were broken open and rifled of their contents. Such articles as could not be made available were thrown into the streets and the torch applied to the house.

Liquors were eagerly sought after and were found in profusion. Barrels of the stuff were rolled into the streets, the heads broken in; then all could indulge without stint or restraint. Wines of a hundred years' vintage met with the same fate.

They were no respecters of person; ornaments were snatched from the persons of delicate females, and " woe unto him " who displayed a watch, fob, or gold chain, as he would be relieved of it 'in short order. Even houses of worship were not_respected; the sacred vessels of the churches were appropriated by the drunken mob. Sacrilege ran riot!

As night approached the destruction became more fierce and unrestrained. Valuable;"cabinets, elegant pianos, costly paintings (many of them im-

ported from foreign lands, the work of some of the
great masters), were ruthlessly smashed to pieces.

By 12 o'clock the city was one great sea of fire!

From the position we occupied, the frightful conflagration seemed like the eruption of an hundred
volcanoes, sending forth their lurid glare and light-
ing the horizon for miles around. Wreaths of flame
shot upward and mingled with the clouds.

It was while gazing on this terrible scene that
my mind turned to our friends in the doomed city.
It seemed impossible that they could escape, even
had the officer reached them in time. Then he
might have been absent, and failed to receive my
communication. The soldier I had sent to carry out
the last item of the program, where was he? It
was time he had reported; something serious might
have happened to him. I cherished for him the
warmest love and friendship, for we had fought, side
by side for four long years in this bloody strife.

While these sad reflections were passing in rapid
succession across my mind, my reverie was suddenly
interrupted by a tap on the shoulder which caused me
to give a sudden start and glance around. It was
the trusted soldier, who had just returned from his
perilous mission. I grasped his hand, and he exclaimed, in the language of Sir Walter Scott:

> " By many a deathbed I have been,
> And many a dying soldier seen,
> But never aught like this."

My first question was, How is it with our friends
in the city?

" All right at 10 o'clock, when I left. The house

was well guarded and the inmates being protected." With that he handed me an envelope addressed in a delicate female hand. We stirred up the smoldering embers of our camp fire, added a few lightwood splinters to make a light; and I proceeded to devour the contents of the missive. The lady began by saying that fortunately the officer to whom I had written was at the front, when the mayor's party met Sherman's advance at the outer edge of the city, so there was no delay in his receiving it.

"It was not long after your party left," she went on to say, "that we heard the unearthly shrieks and " yells of the infuriated soldiers as they came swarm- " ing into the lower part of the city.

" No one will ever know what agony of suspense " we endured as we saw the flames from the burning " buildings ascending heavenward. Our lovely city " was doomed.

" My poor, helpless mother and the wounded soldier " were uppermost in my mind. I wrung my hands " with grief when I realized how utterly helpless we " were to relieve them. I felt that all was lost.

" While in this terrible state of excitement, four " Federals rode up to our front gate; one of them dis- " mounted and threw his reins to one whom I took " to be an orderly. I saw from his garb that he was " an officer. He came directly up the walk to the " front veranda. Then my heart jumped into my " throat. I was terribly agitated. A thousand " thoughts flashed through my mind in an instant. " Summoning all the courage possible, I met him at " the door. His courteous and gentlemanly address

11 b g

"at once subdued my fears.   He handed me his card,
"and in gentle tones asked if there was a wounded
"Confederate soldier in the house.   I told him there
"was.   He politely requested to be shown to his
"room, and I escorted him to the apartment.   He ex-
"pressed much sympathy for the soldier and was
"glad to know that he was so comfortably provided
"for and assured him that he would not want for at-
"tention while the city was occupied, and that he
"need have no apprehension that he would be mo-
"lested.   Then he turned to me and remarked that
"he had but few moments to tarry, but that I might
"rest easy, as the house would be placed under an
"ample guard as soon as the detail could be made.   I
"can but admit that I was somewhat mystified as to
"the proceedings; he must have noticed my quandary,
"for as he arose to depart he remarked that the occa-
"sion furnished him an opportunity, partially, to re-
"ciprocate a kindness extended to him by the one
"making the request that the house and its inmates
"be protected; one for whom he entertained a warm
"and cherished friendship of long standing.   He
"made no further explanation, but bowed himself
"out, mounted his horse and rode off with his com-
"panions.

"In a very short time after they left, twelve Fede-
"ral soldiers, with an officer, rode up to the house.
"The officer in command informed me that he was
"ordered to take possession of the premises and allow
"nothing to be molested.   He also informed me that
"the house was to be designated as 'headquarters'
"for one of the generals, the better to enable them

" to protect it. They seemed to be quiet, genteel,
" well-behaved men. I understand they are from one
" of the Western States—Ohio, I believe.

" P. S., 10 O'CLOCK, P. M. Just received the sig-
" nal of the messenger. Terrible! terrible indeed are
" the surroundings! Our lovely city is in flames!
" How can we ever repay you for the kindness you
" have extended to us? God bless and protect the
" bearer of this on his perilous trip. The distance is
" short, yet he has a great risk to run and many
" dangers to encounter.

" Our guard is standing firm in the midst of this
" terrible conflagration, robbery and destruction that
" is going on about us."

The besotted condition of the Federals who were
plundering the town, was an advantage to the soldier
in carrying out his mission. It was exceedingly
gratifying to me to know that he had passed through
such a reign of terror in safety.

I desire just here to mention in extenuation of the
many atrocities committed by the Federal troops at
Columbia and elsewhere, that the brutality of the
men was largely confined to the foreign element in
the army. The Western troops displayed a much
higher standard of morals and a loftier grade of principle. It was the dregs of the large cities and the
scum of Europe, who seemed utterly void of all the
instincts of humanity; those who joined the Federal
army for plunder and to gratify their inhuman lusts.
Principle with that class of soldiers was an unknown
quality.

CHAPTER XIX.

THE EVACUATION OF CHARLESTON—THE CITY AN
INDESCRIBABLE WRECK—ITS INHABITANTS IN
THE MOST ABJECT DESTITUTION—JOHNSTON
AGAIN IN COMMAND—HIS ARMY BUT A SKIRMISH
LINE—BENTONVILLE—THE SURRENDER—LIN-
COLN'S DEATH.

The fall of Columbia necessitated the evacuation of
Charleston.

General Hardee, who was in command of the Confederate forces at Charleston set fire to all the ware-
houses, where cotton was stored when he left the
place. The fire spread rapidly and ignited a large
lot of powder which was in the depot of the N. E. railroad, causing the loss of over two hundred lives. An
eye witness to the appearance of Charleston after the
troops withdrew, says: "No pen, no pencil, no
" tongue can do justice to the scene; no imagination
"can conceive the complete wreck, the universal ruin,
"the utter desolation. Ruin! ruin!! ruin!!! Above
"and below, on the right hand, on the left hand; ruin,
" ruin everywhere staring at us from every paneless
" window; looking out upon us from every shell-torn
" wall, glaring at us from every battered door,
" pillar and veranda, crouching beneath our feet,
"on every sidewalk. Not Pompeii nor Hercu-
" laneum, nor the Nile, has ruins so saddening, so
" plaintively eloquent."

Other witnesses corroborated this eloquent picture
of the terrible destruction in that beautiful " City by
the Sea."

This left South Carolina in the iron grasp of the Federal army. There she lay, prostrate at the feet of the conqueror. All this devastation of property incident to Sherman's march through the Palmetto State, and the evacuation of Charleston, could have been avoided if the very liberal terms, proposed by Mr. Lincoln at Hampton Roads, had been accepted.

Johnston was again called upon to take command of the Confederate forces in front of Sherman, but his magnificent squadrons had dwindled down to ,the veriest skeleton of an army. But he gathered its scattered fragments together, and once more threw himself in front of Sherman's advancing columns, flushed with bloodless victory. A fierce engagement took place at Bentonville, N. C. It was maintained with the same old-time vigor for several hours. Johnston was forced to give way to a vastly superior force and fall back in the direction of Raleigh.

This was the last battle fought by General Johnston.

Sherman moved slowly and cautiously, feeling his way at every step, well knowing the adroit strategic capability of his old antagonist.

While in the vicinity of Raleigh, and making preparations for its defense, news reached us that Lee had surrendered.

The curtain had fallen on the last act in the great Confederate drama of four years' duration.

General Johnston, satisfied that further resistance was useless, at once entered into negotiations with General Sherman for the surrender of his army. The first interview between the two distinguished officers,

Johnston and Sherman, resulted in a basis of agreement, showing a very liberal and generous disposition on the part of General Sherman toward a gallant but fallen adversary. The stipulations were as follows:

I. The contending armies, now in the field, to maintain their *status quo* until notice is given by the commanding General of either one to its opponent, and reasonable time, say forty-eight hours, allowed.

II. The Confederate armies, now in existence, to be disbanded and conducted to the several State capitals, and there to deposit their arms and public property in the State arsenal; and each officer and man to execute and file an agreement to cease from all acts of war, and abide the action of both State and Federal authorities. The number of arms and munitions of war to be reported to the Chief of Ordnance at Washington City, subject to the future action of the Congress of the United States, and in the meantime to be used solely to maintain peace and order within the borders of the States respectively.

III. The recognition, by the Executive of the United States, of the several State governments, when their officers and legislatures took the oath prescribed by the Constitution of the United States; and, where conflicting State governments have resulted from the war, the legitimacy of all shall be submitted to the Supreme Court of the United States.

IV. The re-establishment of all Federal courts in the several States, with powers as defined by the Constitution and the laws of Congress.

V. The inhabitants of all the States to be guaranteed, so far as the Executive can, their political rights and franchises, as well as their rights of person and property, as defined by the Constitution of the United States, and of the States respectively.

VI. The Executive authority of the United States not to disturb any of the people, by reason of the late war, so long as they live in peace and quiet, abstain from acts of armed hostility, and obey the laws in existence at the place of their residence.

VII. In general terms it announced that: The war is to cease; a general amnesty, so far as the Executive power of the United States can command, on condition of the disbandment of the Federal armies, the distribution of arms and the resumption of peaceful pursuits by officers and men hitherto composing the said armies. Not being fully empowered by our respective principals to fulfil these terms we individually and officially pledge ourselves to promptly obtain necessary authority and to carry out the above program.

The President declined to approve of General Sherman's agreement. This created a lively controversy in Washington.

The following, however, are the terms of capitulation, entered into by the two commanding Generals, on the 26th of April, 1865. It was near Durham, N. C., and disbanded Johnston's army:

All acts of war on the part of the troops under General Johnston's command to cease from this date. All arms and public property to be deposited at Greensboro, and delivered to an Ordnance officer of the United States army. Rolls of all the officers and men to be made in duplicate. One copy to be re-

tained by the commander of the troops, and the other
to be given to an officer designated by General Sherman. Each officer and man to give his individual .
obligation in writing, not to take up arms against the
Government of the United States until properly
released from this obligation. The side arms and
private horses of officers to be retained by them·
This being done, all the officers and men be permitted
to return to their homes, and they not to be disturbed
by the United States authority so long as they ob-
serve their obligation and the laws in the place where
they reside.

The above agreement was signed by both Sherman
and Johnston.

While these negotiations were being carried out
the news was flashed over the country that Mr. Lincoln had been assassinated. The whole country was
in commotion! Never before was such a terrible
state of excitement and consternation manifested.
The South was in nowise connected with the diabolical act, but suffered most in consequence of it. It
was a crushing blow to her just at that critical moment. Mr. Lincoln was a kind-hearted, broad-
minded statesman.

His armies had succeeded in stamping out what he
termed "The Rebellion," and there is no doubt that
had he survived the whole force of his giant intellect
and influence would have been directed to restore
peace and quiet to the distracted country, for even at
that time he commanded the respect and confidence
of the Southern people, who believed in his honesty
of purpose and humanity. As time rolled on and

prejudice subsided, it became more and more apparent to the people of the South that they had sustained a great loss in the death of the "Martyred President." His high and noble character and sublime patriotism will ever shine with renewed lustre. Had his wise counsels been heeded there is scarcely a doubt that the prostrate, bleeding South would have been spared the great humiliation which fell to her lot during the dark days of reconstruction, and thousands of her gallant sons who fell in the last hours of the conflict would have been restored to their homes and firesides with millions of her property saved from destruction.

I have no desire to censure any one in authority at that time "Or set down aught in malice." No doubt they were actuated by pure motives and acted as their best wisdom dictated. But grave mistakes were made during the war and no one acquainted with all the facts will pretend to deny that truth.

I will close this chapter by stating that in the humble judgment of the writer, the greatest mistake of all was starting the war, before a single overt act had been committed by the newly-elected President.

CHAPTER XX.

VISIT TO MY FEDERAL FRIEND—HE TELLS OF CO-
LUMBIA—MR. DAVIS AND CABINET—THAT SPECIE
TRAIN—THE LAST CABINET MEETING—MR. DAVIS
CAPTURED—REFLECTIONS.

At the conclusion of Sherman's and Johnston's
agreement for the surrender of the Confederate army,
I decided to visit the Federal camps, hunt up my old
friend, and ascertain the fate of the friends we had
left in such great peril in Columbia on the night of
its destruction. Accompanied by the soldier who
brought the last information from them, I soon
reached the Federal lines. There we were received
with marked courtesy by the " Boys in Blue," who
expressed themselves as delighted to learn that war
was over. We soon reached the quarters of my friend,
where we met, not as on former occasions, when
hopes were bright and expectations high. Both were
battle-scarred and weather-beaten, presenting a far
different appearance from that of four years previous,
when we sat on the banks of the Rio Grande and
discussed the various aspects of the war then in its in-
cipiency. Each grasped the other's hand in a warm
and friendly greeting, not without betraying, however, an emotion it was impossible for either to conceal. A moment elapsed before a word was uttered.
The silence was broken by my friend, who exclaimed
in a tone which indicated its sincerity : " *Thank God !
this cruel war is over !* " After extending to each

other the usual congratulations for our safe delivery from the baptism of fire through which we had passed, I made haste to inquire as to the safety of our friends in Columbia. " All right," he replied. " It " was fortunate for them," he went on to say, " That your communication was not delayed in reach- " ing me. I at once made my request known to the " Commanding General, who, without hesitation, " placed at my disposal an adequate force for their " protection. I found them a refined and cultured " household. The wounded soldier I became very " much interested in, for he was certainly a young " man of more than ordinary intelligence. He was " quite nervous, no doubt, from the apprehension " that he would receive harsh treatment when the " troops got possession of the city.` I quieted him in " that respect, however, by assuring him that there " was no danger of his being molested. I also told " him that there would be no soldiers on the place, " except the guard, who knew their duty and would " carry out their instructions to the letter.

" The house caught fire twice during the night, but " was saved from destruction by the vigilance of the " guard. It was a great advantage that it was situ- " ated somewhat remote from other buildings, as there " was fire on every side.

" The scene witnessed in Columbia that night beg- " gars description! I directed a number of ladies to " the house of your friend, where, I am happy to say, " they remained without molestation. In fact, I, " with some of my fellow-officers, spent the most of " that fearful night, in shielding many of the unfor

"tunate inhabitants from insult and robbery. There
" were atrocities committed in that town too horrible
" for language to express! I am happy to state, how-
" ever, that they were not committed by our American
" soldiers, or sanctioned by our regular army officers.
" The guard was not withdrawn until the last of our
" troops had left the city." I replied that I should
ever feel grateful for the favor.

" Don't say that; for I was exceedingly gratified
" when the opportunity presented itself where I could
" serve you." "I will simply state, Colonel" (that was
his rank), I answered, "that I was well aware that your
" gentlemanly instincts would prompt you to protect a
" lady under any and all circumstances, and I must
" thank you for the promptness with which you re-
" sponded to my request."

During our conversation there was no allusion to
the surrender, further than that we both expressed
ourselves as feeling rejoiced that the war was over,
and that all might return to their homes and resume
the peaceful avocations of life once more.

As a natural consequence, our conversation drifted
to scenes of other days. He informed me that the
object of his heart's cherished affection was still oc-
cupying her quiet retreat, far away, on the banks of
the beautiful Rio Grande; and she was still as true
as the polarity of the needle. He was suffering, at
times, from the effects of his wound, and intended to
apply for a year's leave of absence, when he expected
to visit Europe, and hoped to be accompanied by the
dark-eyed beauty as Mrs. ——.

The two armies had stacked their arms and were

lying side by side. No longer was brother arrayed against brother, or father against son, in deadly conflict. The Federal army was soon to take up its triumphal march to the Nation's Capital, with flags flying and bands discoursing martial airs. They would be received with open arms, amid the shouts and plaudits of a grateful people. On the other hand, the shattered remnants of the Confederate army, with their blood-stained banners trailing in the dust; footsore, weary and broken in spirits; without money and with scarcely sufficient clothing to shield them from the scorching rays of the summer sun; the victors of a hundred battles must scatter singly, or in groups, to make their way as best they could, through a devastated country, to their distant and desolate homes. God, in his infinite wisdom, had decreed against them, and they were forced to bow in humble submission to this stern and immutable decree.

Had I the pen of a Homer, dipped in the fired imagination of a Shakespeare, I would fall far short of depicting in its true colors, the melancholy disruption of the Confederate army, upon that eventful occasion. Brave men, who had stood in the smoke and blaze of battle; scarred veterans, whose place had been in the front for four long years without flinching; men who had remained unblanched amid the carnage of a forlorn hope, gave way to their feelings, and wept like inconsolable children when they grasped each other's hands in a final separation! The Confederacy was dead. The principles for which they struggled so long and for which they had suffered so terribly had been crushed to earth; their banners, which had

waved over so many victorious fields were forever
furled; and posterity would have to vindicate the
rightfulness of their cause.

Mr. Davis, with his cabinet, were not included in
the terms of the surrender, and they were endeavor-
ing to make their way out of the country.

At Greenville, N. C., Mr. Davis made a speech,
from the balcony of one of the hotels in the place,
in which he stated that an effort would be made to
cross the Mississippi river, and there continue the
struggle. This was looked upon by the soldiers who
heard him, as a hopeless and visionary scheme. All
realized that the war had closed; and regarded it as
the height of folly to continue the contest longer in
any part of the country.

The last cabinet meeting of the Confederacy was
held in the front yard of a country house, near the
town of Washington, Wilkes County, Georgia. This
meeting was held for the purpose of devising the best
and safest plan to avoid capture. They were well
aware of the fact that if they fell into the hands of
the enemy, they would be thrown into prison and remain there indefinitely.

An animated discussion arose between Mr. Davis
and General John C. Breckenridge, his Secretary of
War, on this subject. General Breckenridge con-
tended that it was extremely hazardous to continue
in a westerly direction, as it was almost certain to
result in their capture. These two gentlemen failed
to agree upon any plan; consequently, General Breckenridge selected a few friends, his young son, Cabel,
being one of the number, took a due south course

and made their way, as rapidly as possible, regardless of roads, to a point on the coast of Florida, where they secured a small boat and escaped to the island of Cuba; from whence they took shipping for Europe, where they arrived in safety.

Mr. Davis, with his family and the remaining members of his cabinet, continued their western course, and were captured near Macon, Ga. His capture and subsequent imprisonment have been graphically described in a little volume, entitled "Prison Life of Jefferson Davis, by Brevet Lieutenant-Colonel John J. Craven, M.D., Surgeon United States Volunteers, and physician of the distinguished prisoner during his confinement in Fortress Monroe, from May 25th, 1865, to December 25th, 1865."

Had Mr. Davis and party accompanied General Breckenridge the South would have escaped the humiliating spectacle of seeing their chieftain loaded with irons and thrown into a dungeon, a horrible outrage, which the following lines from an unknown author depict in as glowingly and eloquent language, as if uttered by the manacled President himself:

MANACLED.

"Stop, soldier! This cruel act
    Will ring through all the land!
Shame on the heart that planned the deed!
    Shame on the coward hand
That drops the sword of justice bright,
    To grasp these iron rings!
On them, not me, dishonor falls!
    To them this dark shame clings.

Manacled! O, my God! my God!
Is this a Christian land?
And did our countries ever meet
And grasp each other's hand?
O, Mexico! on thy red fields
I battled midst the fray!
My riflemen, with steady aim,
Won Buena Vista's day!

Manacled! far down the South
Let this one word speed fast;
My country! thou hast borne great wrongs,
But this, the last, the last,
Will send a thrill through thy high heart;
Despair will spurn control,
And these hard irons pressing *here*,
Will enter thy proud soul!

Manacled! O, word of shame!
Ring it through all the world!
My countrymen! on you, on you
This heavy wrong is hurled!
We flung our banners to the air;
We fought as brave men fight;
Our battle-cry rang through the land,
Home! Liberty! and Right!

Manacled! for this I am here,
Clanking the prisoner's chain—
We fought—and nobly did we fight—
We fought, but fought in vain;
Down in that billowy sea of blood,
Went all our jewels rare!
And hope rushed wailing from the scene
And took herself to prayer!

Manacled! Manacled! words of woe,
But words of greater shame;
I've that within me which these wrongs
Can never, never tame;
And standing proud in conscious worth,
I represent my land,
And that 'Lost Cause' for which she bled,
Lofty   Heroic! Grand!"

When Richmond was evacuated a large amount of specie was shipped out by rail, variously estimated at from $1,000,000 to $3,000,000. It consisted of gold and silver coin, the gold being packed in ammunition boxes and the silver in kegs. It was generally understood at the time that a large portion of this money belonged to the banks in Richmond, and the balance belonged to the Confederate Government, which was then virtually a defunct institution. This specie was taken from the train at a point in North Carolina, the name of which I cannot recall; loaded on wagons and transported under a strong guard to Washington, Ga. At that point the gold was, by order of General Breckenridge, deposited in the cellar of a private house for safe keeping. What ultimately became of it the writer never knew. A portion of the silver was divided among the train escort, which consisted of portions of Ferguson's, Vaughn's and Duke's brigades. The balance of the specie fell into the hands of the Federals. The Confederates received from two to three dollars each. This was a meager amount to defray their expenses home, taking into consideration the distance most of them had to travel. But, to the everlasting credit of the Southern people, they never refused to divide their last morsel with the returning Confederate soldier.

Never before in the history of the world have the disbanded troops of two great armies returned to the peaceful pursuits of civil life with so little disturbance. They were tired of war, and it took them but a very short time to settle down to the avocations of civil life, it was hard to distinguish the ex-soldiers from the citizens.

12 b g

CHAPTER XXI.

BLOCKADE RUNNING—WHAT LED TO IT—SEMINOLE
CHASES THE SUSANNA—A GRAPHIC ACCOUNT—
CAPTAIN AUSTIN—THAT CONFEDERATE COTTON

In this chapter I will treat of that branch of the Confederate service which has heretofore been so much overlooked in making up the history of the great " War Between the States."

With the limited resources at the command of the South for carrying on so stupendous a struggle it was necessary she should resort to every expedient known to the rules of war to obtain supplies and munitions of war to keep up her armies. Her ports were blockaded, necessarily cutting off all direct communication with foreign countries. Her only mediums of exchange on which the South could rely were her cotton and naval stores. Of these she had an almost unlimited supply, and they commanded good prices in the markets of the old world. The only way to make these available was to pass them through her blockaded ports, which was a dangerous and perilous undertaking.

In order to make blockade running a success it was necessary to engage the very best marine talent. It not only required men of nerve and sagacity, but they must be expert navigators, with a thorough knowledge of all the approaches to the ports along the southern lines of sea and Gulf coast. It will at once be seen that the blockade runner became an im-

portant factor in the problem of Confederate com-
merce." Staunch and fast-sailing vessels were constructed for the purpose.

One of the most successful commanders in these
hazardous expeditions was Captain Charles W. Austin, who, at the breaking out of the war, was in command of one of the " Harris and Morgan Line " of
steamships, plying between the ports of Galveston,
Tex., and New Orleans, La. He was a thorough seaman and an accomplished navigator, at home on the
deck of a ship; always cool and collected under the
most trying and adverse circumstances. These were
all evidenced in a most miraculous escape he made off
Galveston harbor, when hotly pursued by the U. S.
steamship-of-war, Seminole. The account given below was written at the time by Captain J. F. Mackie,
an officer on board the Seminole during the chase :

" A STRIKING CHASE AT SEA.

" *The Remarkable Escape of a Confederate Privateer, off Galveston Harbor, in 1865.*

" We were now within less than two miles of the
" flying stranger, when we opened fire upon her from
" our eleven-inch pivot, exploding a shell right under
" her bow, and nearly deluging the steamer's deck
" with water, but doing no further harm. While we
" were reloading the pivot, she put helm hard-a-star-
" board and ran across our bow, heading directly for
" the shore (distant about a mile and a half), appa-
" rently intending to run herself ashore. Captain
" Clarey shouted : ' Put yourself hard-a-starboard,
" sir.' ' Hard-a-starboard, sir,' answered the officer

" at the wheel, at the same moment putting the wheel
" sharply about, and the ship turned on her keel, as
" if she knew what was expected of her, and started
" directly for the shore with the steamer now right
" abeam (starboard side), about a mile off, bringing
" our whole battery of five guns to bear on her.
" The captain called out to ' Forward rifle! Fire as
" soon as you are ready and without further orders,
" only don't waste the ammunition.'

" ' Pivot there, sir; fire carefully and aim at the
" wheel-house, and at no other place. Sink her, if
" possible; go ahead and show us what you can do.'

" ' Quarter-deck battery: take good aim at the
" wheel-house; don't let her get away from us.'

" A shell from the rifle exploded over her; a shell
" from the eleven-inch bursted close beside her, and
" the three and eight-inch shell guns were sending
" their compliments thick and fast, but, strange to
" say, not a single shell had struck her! She seemed
" to bear a charmed life. We were about half a mile
" distant from each other, and about a mile from the
" shore, when she suddenly changed her course to
" south-southwest, and started to run along the coast,
" heading directly for us. At the same instant the
" lead man in the chains cried out:

" ' By the deep three fathoms!'

" ' Hard-a-starboard, quartermaster!' cried Captain
" Clarey, and as the ship's head swung to port, he re-
" marked ' By —— ! we'd been ashore in another
" second!' The Seminole was drawing sixteen feet
" and deep at that.

" It was now nip and tuck. The stranger was going

" to run for it, and the bar was between us. Our only
" chance was to sink her before she got in. The most
" intense excitement prevailed on board each vessel.
" Captain Clarey raved and swore and stamped, but
" all to no effect. Shot after shot went over and ex-
" ploded beyond, on the shore. We were now rapidly
" approaching Galveston harbor, and it seemed as if
" she was going to get away in spite of us. Her
" captain, for the last hour, had been walking the
" bridge between the wheel-houses, with both hands in
" the pockets of his pea-jacket, smoking a cigar very
" unconcernedly; but that there was a feeling that
" their lives and property hung only on a single
" thread, was manifest by the way those wheels flew
" around, leaving a track of boiling, foamy sea far
" astern; and the huge volumes of black smoke that
" poured out of the funnels told a story that it did not
" need a trumpet to announce.

" The channel now began to widen, and if she could
" only hold her own for twenty minutes she would
" escape. What must have been the thoughts of that
" captain, as he walked to and fro on that bridge with
" the air full of flying missiles, now hid in the smoke,
" again in a second or two, one flying missile a few
" feet above his head; the next minute drenched with
" their spray! He *never flinched or changed his man-*
" *ner*, but kept quietly on as if it were an every-day
" affair.

" The sight was one of the most picturesque I ever
" witnessed. The fleet, about two miles below, look-
" ing with eager eyes to see us sink the flying stranger;
" the bay gradually widening, with the white sand

"hills in the distance, the city of Galveston to the
"south, its piers filled with sympathetic spectators;
"the fort in the bay, with the Confederate flag flying,
"and its ramparts crowded with men watching and
"praying for the success of the flying stranger; the
"three steamers flying through the water like hounds,
"ofttimes hidden by the smoke of their guns, as they
"were loaded and fired.   But fate decided in favor of
"the flying stranger.   In spite of our every effort to
"prevent her, she reached the bay of Galveston.   The
"bay is nearly three miles wide and the channel is
"very dangerous to vessels drawing more than ten
"feet of water; and as we were getting into three
"fathoms again, with intense chagrin we gave up the
"chase, sending as a parting compliment an eleven-
"inch shell, with our *regrets*."

In connection with the above, I give a statement
made by Captain Austin himself, to a reporter of the
Savannah *Sunday Telegraph*, which was published in
that paper November 18, 1883, and was headed, "A
Blockader's Last Run."   It relates to the remarkable
escape and final capture of the Confederate steamer
Susanna, and is thus given.   Every word in both
accounts is authentic:

"'It was about 11 o'clock in the forenoon, some-
"time along in the fall of 1864, in the month of
"October, I think, that I ran the Federal blockade
"into Galveston harbor, in command of the steamer
"Susanna, with a cargo of arms and ammunition, for
"the Confederate government.'

"The speaker was a medium-sized, square-built
"man with deep-set eyes and determined features. 'I

" have read the account in the *Sunday News,*' he con-
" tinued, 'of the striking chase at sea and
" remarkable escape of a Confederate steamer at Gal-
" veston. I was in command 'of that ship at that
" time.' The reporter at once recognized an old
" Savannah man, Captain Charles W. Austin, who is
" now in the employ of the government, and who
" figured in many thrilling adventures during the
" war, but came out without a scar.

" You had a narrow escape, Captain, tell us some-
" thing about the affair.

"' As I said, it was sometime in the fall of '64.
" I had made four or five successful trips from Ha-
" vana, bringing arms and munitions of war, but
" this trip pretty nearly wound me up. The Susanna,
" which the writer in the *News* referred to as ' the
" privateer,' was a staunch, trim iron vessel, with a
" capacity of from 1,400 to 1,800 bales of cotton,
" and with an average speed of fifteen knots an hour.
" She was built in Scotland, on the Clyde, as a block-
" ade runner. She lay low in the water, with her
" long black hulk hardly visible, except in broad day-
" light. She was about 225 feet long by 30 feet beam,
" and being a new vessel I felt her equal to anything
" in a chase.

"' We left Havana with a crew of twenty-seven
" men, well officered, and with men who knew their
" business. We had fine weather, and calculated to
" make land inside the blockade, under cover of night,
" between one and five o'clock in the morning. How-
" ever, as luck would have it, an accident at sea, the
" giving way of some of our machinery, detained us

"several hours, and brought us to land in open day-
"light, about six o'clock in the morning. By this
"time we were in plain sight of the blockading
"squadron; but, as yet, we were unobserved. The
"entrance to the harbor was filled with gunboats.
"It was near the close of the war, and the blockade
"at other points on the coast having been raised
"nearly all the Federal cruisers were concentrated at
"Galveston. The situation was a perilous one, and
"there was but one thing left to be done. If we
"could evade the enemy until nightfall, and then
"pass the squadron and enter the harbor unobserved,
"we would be all right.

"'Calling the men aft, to the bridge, I gave them
"their orders, and the ship was soon heading toward
"land. We stood to the eastward, close under shore,
"with the intention of secreting ourselves until
"night. We were yet some distance out and hauling
"in rapidly, when about eight o'clock I discovered a
"cruiser bearing down upon us. All hope of making
"land was then abandoned, and the only chance of
"escape was to put out to sea. Having full confi-
"dence in my men, and knowing the speed of my
"ship, I did not fear the result. Calling to the engi-
"neer through the pipe, I discovered that, after
"making twelve hours' run of shore and back again,
"I would not have coal enough to carry me back to
"Havana. As there was none to be had in Galves-
"ton, I was in a quandary; but no time was to be
"lost. 'Give her full head,' I shouted to the engi-
"neer, and casting my glass across the water, I saw
"that the Federal cruiser was preparing for action.

" There was only one alternative, and in forlorn hope
" I took the desperate chance of running the squadron
" and beaching the blockader. It was then about
" noon. I headed the ship for Galveston and passed
" over the outer bar into the swash, or beach chan-
" nel. We were hauling in south by west, in the very
" teeth of the guns on the gunboat Seminole, which
" had already opened fire. At this point the chase
" began, and for an hour we ran under the heavy fire
" from the guns of THREE of the squadron, which
" were bearing down on us all the time.

" ' Push her hard,' I shouted again to the engineer·
" 'All right, sir,' came the reply, and the huge, black
" volumes of smoke which poured out of our funnels
" and lay in clouds on the water, the throbbing of
" the engine in the hold, the streaming of the wheels,
" as they flew around, plowing the water and leav-
" ing a huge track of boiling, foaming sea far astern,
" all told he was doing his duty. It was an exciting
" time, but every man was at his post and not a word
" was spoken. The shells whizzed over us and
" splashed and drenched our decks, as they fell close
" under our sides. Two solid shots passed through
" our funnels, as I stood on the bridge, and the frag-
" ments of a shell shattered our bow above water,
" but otherwise we were unhurt. I could watch the
" movements of the men of the cruiser through my
" glass, as I stood on the bridge, between the flashes
" of their guns and the clearing away of the smoke.
" We were, even now, about half a mile distant from
" each other, and a mile distant from the shore.

" 'All right below?' I inquired again through the

"" pipe. 'All right, sir,' again was the answer, and
" the ship rushed on, as the shot fell thick and fast,
" but the chase was about up. The bar was between
" us and the gunboats, and the distance grew greater
" as the channel widened. In ten minutes we would
" be out of her reach; and running the ship under
" Pelican Point, we were under cover of our own guns
" and sheltered from the enemy's fire.

"'We were now safe; the open bay lay before us,
" with the white sand hills beyond; the fleet was lying
" about two miles below, and the fort and wharves
" along the city were lined with thousands of specta-
" tors, who had witnessed the chase and who received
" us with open arms.

"'It was a " nip-and-tuck " race, captain,' remarked
" the reporter. 'How did you feel with the shells
" bursting about you?' 'Well, about as I do now,'
" was the reply, as the complacent captain stood with
" his hands in his pockets, quietly smoking a cigar.
"'True, there was about two hundred tons of pow-
" der under the bridge; but it's all in a lifetime and
" there's no use getting excited.

"'We lay in port about eighteen days discharging
" our cargo and reloading with cotton, when we again
" put to sea, and passed the squadron without being
" molested. Everything went smooth, until about
" sixty miles off Cuba, when we broke our crank pin
" and were so disabled, we were picked up by the
" Federal ship, Metacomy, commanded by Captain
" Jewett, and taken to Philadelphia. I was tried
" there, and the Susanna was condemned as a govern-
" ment prize.'"

It is stated by the citizens of Galveston that Captain Austin rarely ever failed to come in on regular time, and many are the exciting scenes they relate, as having witnessed between the gallant captain and the blockading squadron.

The successful running of the blockade afforded the Confederate government an opportunity for landing large lots of cotton in European ports, which formed a basis of credit and enabled her to fit out privateers and equip a very respectable little navy.

Much of the Confederate cotton that was stored in Europe, at the close of the war, fell into private hands and developed shortly after the war into large private fortunes for individuals, who had always been known before to be either indigent or only in moderate circumstances. These are, to-day, living in ease and even luxury. Such has always been the result of war; the few will prosper at the expense of the many. Patriotism, with some, becomes a secondary consideration, when money is the issue. This cotton, by right belonged to the United States government, as the legitimate results of the war.

CHAPTER XXII.

CAPTAIN AUSTIN CAPTURES THE UNITED STATES
TRANSPORT FOX—THE RAM MANASSAS—SHE AT-
TACKS THE BLOCKADING SQUADRON—IS PUR-
CHASED BY THE CONFEDERATE GOVERNMENT.

One of the most daring and perilous exploits that
occurred during the war, in which Captain Austin
was the central figure, occurred off Mobile harbor,
and threw the city into great commotion and excitement ; no account of which has ever been given to
the public.   It formed an era in the eventful life of
that daring and intrepid seaman; and should be a
matter of historic record, as it pertained so vitally to
the cause for which he fought.   The following circumstances of the gallant achievement were related
to the writer by an old and highly respected citizen of
Mobile.

The steamship Fox, a large government transport,
was employed by the United States government to
furnish supplies to the blockading squadrons along
the Gulf Coast.   On the occasion referred to, she had
discharged her cargo and was quietly lying at anchor,
under cover of the guns of the|blockaders at Mobile.
Captain Austin chanced to be in Mobile at the time
and conceived an idea for her capture.   Quietly and
unobserved he secured a spot where, with a pair of
strong marine glasses he could locate her exactly.
Becoming satisfied that he could secure the prize, he
returned to Mobile to perfect his plans.

He secured a ship's yawl boat, with six brave and determined men, for the dangerous adventure.

With muffled oars they quietly made their way along in the shadow of the land, until they were opposite the transport, which lay at anchor about a mile off shore.

The night was favorable for their operations. The Gulf was as smooth as a rippling stream; and those speechless watchers of the night, that shone out so brightly overhead, gave no warning to the slumbering crew on board the doomed ship, that an enemy was near.

Unobserved by the single sentry on watch they made their way to the ship's side, and in less time than it takes to write it Captain Austin, followed by six determined men, had climbed over the forechains, secured the man on watch, and the ship was in their possession.

It took but a moment for Captain Austin to determine his course. He placed the officers and crew under guard, in the cabin, slipped the anchor, and, with a fair head of steam (which is always kept up on these vessels), he headed the ship for Mobile harbor.

He was compelled to pass close under the guns of two of the blockaders, who hailed him to know what ship it was, and whither bound, to which he replied: "United States Transport Fox; bound for Key West." Without further questioning, he was allowed to pass, and reached Mobile a little after sunrise.

The news of the capture spread rapidly. The

city was soon astir; and the excitement ran high.
Captain Austin and his little band were applauded as
benefactors, intrepid men—heroes! The citizens of
Mobile gave them a grand ovation; opened wide the
gates of the city and bade them welcome. Captain
Austin was presented with a handsome gold watch
and chain, on which this daring act was inscribed, as
a token of their appreciation and respect.

The ship proved a valuable prize and was turned
over to the Confederate authorities.

Another historic event, in which Captain Austin
was a conspicuous actor, took place on the Mississippi
river in the early part of the war; an account of
which was given in the *New York World* May 6th,
1883; and was afterwards published in the *Savannah
Teleglraph*:

"THE RAM MANASSAS."

"The history of the 'Ram Manassas,' and of her
" projector and commander, should be placed on
" record before it is too late to get the truth.

" John A. Stephenson, a wealthy retired sea captain,
" was living in New Orleans at the breaking out of
" the civil war, and the Manassas was wholly his
" conception and invention, and it was put afloat en-
" tirely at his expense.

" Before the battle of ' Bull Run ' he purchased the
" ' Enoch Train,' which had been constructed in Bos-
" ton, and used as a tow-boat on the Mississippi river.
" She was a double propeller, with two engines and
" powerful machinery. She was one hundred and
" eighty feet long, twenty-two feet abeam, eight feet

"hold, and about ninety-six tons burden. He took
"off her house, cut her to her plank-shears, and then
"first put on an arched deck of heavy timber, com-
"pletely covering her from stem to stern, in the shape
"of a turtle's back; finally plating the whole with
"two thicknesses of railroad iron, bent and fitted so
"as to form a smooth surface over the whole outside
"to the water's edge; two short smokestacks alone
"protruded above the even surface of the whole out-
"side. The prow was constructed with heavy iron,
"projecting in front about five feet, and three and a
"half feet under water. She was steered by a wheel
"entirely covered under the deck. In case she should
"be boarded by an enemy, it was so arranged that
"hot water could be thrown in streams upon the board-
"ing party.

"The construction of such a novelty at New Or-
"leans attracted public attention. It was visited by
"many hundreds of people, and was known as the
"'Nondescript,' and generally ridiculed; but Stephen-
"son was strong minded, had faith and money, and
"was encouraged by his friends. Captain Charles
"W. Austin, now a resident of Savannah, Ga., super-
"intended her construction, and from him all the
"facts herein mentioned were obtained.

"When completed, which was soon after the battle
"of 'Bull Run,' the next thing was to obtain a crew.

"Federal gunboats, heavily armed, were lying at
"the mouth of the Mississippi; and it was these it
"was intended she should attack.

"Commodore Hollins, the Confederate Naval Com-
"mander at New Orleans, refused to detail men for

" service in her, but gave consent to Captain Austin
" to obtain volunteers, if he could get them ; and
" nineteen men were obtained. With these the Ma-
" nassas proceeded to Fort Jackson, twenty-two miles
" above the blockading squadron. Commodore Hol-
" lins allowed Stephenson and Austin the use of his
" dispatch boat ' Iva,' with which to reconnoiter the
" enemy in the afternoon preparatory to a night at-
" tack.   They approached to a point just out of range.
" There lay the steam sloop-of-war Richmond, next
" to the east bank of the river, with twenty-two guns;
" then the sloop of war Vintimus, with fourteen guns;
" and next, the steam sloop-of-war Waterwitch, with
" six guns.   They all lay abreast, across the Missis-
" sippi, at the head of the passes.   They were headed
" up stream, with their springs out, guns shotted ; all
" ready for action at a moment's notice.

"These four Federal boats, with fifty-six guns,
" were a mighty power for the single ' Nondescript,'
" with nineteen heroes and NO GUNS, to attack.

"Some of the Confederate naval officers had said
" that the ' Nondescript ' would be blown out of the
" water.

"Leaving Fort Jackson at about eight o'clock on
" the morning of October 12th, 1861, with Captain
" Austin, her commander, as the only man on deck,
" and each of his men at their proper places below,
" the ' Ram ' proceeded to and arrived at the scene of
" action about three o'clock in the morning.   The
" Richmond had been selected by Captain Austin, in
" the afternoon, as the Federal boat first to be attacked.
" Nearing the Richmond, the ' Nondescript ' was put

" under the utmost headway, and not until it was too
" late to withdraw without discomfiture, perhaps disas-
" ter, was it discovered that a schooner was lying along-
" side of the Richmond, on the side of the attack.
" The ram proceeded, all steam on, and, striking the
" schooner first, cut her in two, and ran the iron prow
" of the 'Nondescript' clear into the Richmond. The
" ram then hauled off and the schooner sank. The
" Richmond discharged her broadside at the ram, but
" without effect. The Richmond found herself dis-
" abled and leaking ; and giving signals of danger to
" the other vessels of the blockading squadron, all
" disappeared down the passes."

The blow which the ram struck the schooner and
the Richmond produced such concussion as to dis-
able one of her engines and render her unfit to
attempt further aggression ; but it did not cause
Captain Austin to lose his footing on the deck.

The ram was neither aided nor followed by any
fire-rafts, or any steamer or propeller astern of her ;
nor were any shells thrown, or guns fired at the
Federal fleet, as some Federal accounts have stated.

The ram was taken back to New Orleans and repaired ; was adopted by the Confederate authorities,
and Mr. Stephenson fully compensated for her.

The "Nondescript" was named the "Manassas" by
Stephenson, soon after the battle of Bull Run.

The Confederacy having been thus taught how to
build effective war vessels, then, and not until then,
began the changing of the Merrimac into an iron-
clad ram, at Norfolk, Va. Mr. Stephenson, in build-

13 b g

ing the Manassas, builded wiser than he knew; for
in a practical way, he gave to the world new ideas as
to warship building and the carrying on of naval
warfare, which have since revolutionized the navies of
the world.

CHAPTER XXIII.

A short sketch of the life of one who figured so conspicuously in Confederate marine affairs during the war, and of whom so little has ever been said or written, will be instructive and interesting to the reader and exceedingly gratifying to his many friends who survive him.

Captain Charles William Austin was descended from staunch old New England stock of Scotch origin, and the name is identified with the early history of this country. His ancestors took a conspicuous part in the great American revolution, one of his relatives, Roger Sherman, being one of the signers of the Declaration of Independence. His grandfather, John P. Austin, graduated at Yale college with distinction and died in Texas in 1836, where the family name became identified with the early history of that republic, now a state, which is an empire within herself.

The subject of this brief memoir, in early life developed a taste for the sea. He inherited a roving disposition and for a number of years was connected with the United States navy.

For several years previous to the great Civil war, he was connected with the merchant marine, and commanded some of the finest ships then afloat.

He was a thorough seaman in every sense of the

(195)

word; a man of keen perception and penetrating sagacity; mild and pleasing in his deportment, but stern and exacting in the discharge of duty. He knew no such word as *fear*. If there was any touch of pride or vanity in his make-up it was only perceptible while walking the deck of his ship as she plowed majestically through the billows of the deep. He neither became excited nor lost his mental equilibrium under the most trying circumstances.

His long experience at sea, with his wide geographical knowledge, rendered his services of the utmost importance to the Confederacy.

The South had no navy; therefore blockade running became the principal theater of his operations. A few instances in this perilous enterprise have already been noted, and the following account of his escape from Fort Taylor can but be of thrilling interest to the reader:

CAPTAIN AUSTIN'S ESCAPE FROM FORT TAYLOR.

There are very many instances recorded of daring, even desperate courage and almost miraculous escapes from death, and escapes from captivity which evidence a coolness, a courage and an ingenuity, which make us pause in wonder and admiration of man's almost unlimited capacity. The lives of few men who have surprised and even startled the world, have afforded as many evidences of fertility of resources combined with ingenuity and cool, deliberate courage in execution, as can be found in the checkered career of Captain Charles W. Austin. His attack of the blockading fleet off New Orleans, when with the ram, Manassas, without a gun, he single-handed and alone, sunk a schooner, disabled a man-of-war and drove the fleet out to sea. Soon afterwards he conceived the capture of the United States transport, Fox, and in an open yawl he captured and brought her out from under the very guns of the fleet and delivered her in the harbor of Mobile, a prize to the Confederate government. His escape when chased by the fleet off Galveston reads like a romance.

All these have been told, but his escape from Fort Taylor, the climax of his adventures, has remained untold. In 1863 while in the blockade service, Captain Austin was captured and confined in Fort Taylor in the harbor of Key West, Fla. Associating with himself a fellow-prisoner of nerve, Captain Austin formed his plans and patiently awaited the arrival of some merchant vessel that these plans might be carried into execution. One bright morning some weeks after his incarceration, Captain Austin espied a schooner as she dropped anchor some hundred yards from the fort. Her movements and "make-up" were carefully scrutinized, all of which proved satisfactory, particularly as the craft exhibited every evidence of remaining at her moorings until daylight. Darkness approached and with it their time for action. On the water-side of the fort in the cell of Captain Austin, was an aperture left for light and ventilation and large enough to admit of the passage of a man's body. From this aperture to the water was thirty feet. After the sentinel on duty had made his rounds and inspections and had reported, "all right," Captain Austin and his companion began opcrations. From their bedclothes they had constructed a good, strong rope, one end of which they made fast inside of their cell, and the balance of it was thrown out of the aperture. Through the opening and down the rope into the water went the captain, closely followed by his fellow-prisoner. Both men being expert swimmers, soon reached the stern of the schooner and took possession of her yawl. Then noiselessly climbing over the schooner's bow, the captain secured her compass from the binnacle. The schooner's officers and crew were peacefully sleeping, feeling secure under the very guns of the fort. To attempt to get provisions or water would certainly arouse them and bring disaster to our poor Confederates, so the captain descended into the yawl and the two companions began their journey from Key West to Cuba in an open boat, without either water or food.

Beneath the scorching rays of a tropical sun, for forty-eight hours, with not even a drop of water to quench their consuming thirst, their sufferings must be endured to be appreciated. They landed upon a desolate beach, completely prostrated.

Fortunately for them, they were soon discovered by a fisherman who chanced to pass along the beach and who ministered to their necessities, and by careful nursing so resuscitated them as to enable him to get them to his hut, where, under his kindly care they were soon restored to health and strength. From the fisherman's hut they went to Havana, where they fell in with friends and soon were back in Dixie.

Captain Austin, being a man of modest and retiring disposition, would rarely refer to any of his adventures, and then would treat them simply as matters of duty.

He was a commander by nature—a leader of men; and if justice is ever done to his name, he will rank with the most prominent naval commanders of the world. His single act, while in command of the Ram Manassas, has no parallel in the annals of naval warfare. It is not at all likely that the brilliant engagement between the Merrimac and the Monitor, which took place in Hampton Roads, would ever have occurred, had not the little, turtle-backed Manassas, with Captain Austin on her deck, developed the practicability of an iron-clad vessel in a naval engagement. It was a revelation to the naval commanders of the world they had never dreamed of before.

After the war closed Captain Austin went into the service of the " Harris and Morgan Steamship Company," and in a few months after was married to Miss Georgia Grafton, of Galveston, Texas, a lady of culture and refinement, with rare mental attainments.

Captain Austin, shortly after his marriage, retired from the sea and accepted a position from the United States Government. He was employed in deepening and widening the channel, and otherwise improving the harbor of Savannah, Ga. He held that position up to the time of his death, which occurred April 17th, 1889, after a lingering illness, brought on by exposure during the war. He left a wife and three children, two sons and one daughter, to mourn his loss. They all reside in Savannah, where the remains of the heroic husband and father sleep, in close proximity to the broad Atlantic, where her mournful cadence will chant his requiem until the last trump shall summon all hands to quarters.

Some day posterity may do justice to his memory by placing a suitable monument to mark the resting place of the man who commanded the first iron-clad warship of the world. The naval officers of the various nations, if the matter were brought to their notice, would, no doubt, gladly contribute to erect a shaft in the " Monumental city of the South," to perpetuate the name and deeds of the gallant skipper. Peace to his ashes.

CHAPTER XXIV.

RECONSTRUCTION—CARPET-BAGGERS AND SCALA-
WAGS—THEIR INFAMY—SOLDIERS GOOD CITI-
ZENS—CONDITION OF THE SOUTH—THE NEGRO
DURING THE WAR.

The South was invaded by two mighty armies.
One was the "Boys in Blue," whose home was on the
tented field. They had responded to their country's
call, to arbitrate the great question of secession by
force of arms. These were under strict military dis-
cipline. The other army was a heterogeneous mass of
humanity, gathered from the four quarters of the
earth, who, like vultures around a carcass, hung about
the skirts of the Northern armies, as they penetrated
the South, seeking whom and what they might devour. When a battle took place they were always
found skulking in the rear. They were the degen-
erate offspring of a spurious ancestry. Too cowardly
to risk their lives beside the soldiers in the field, they
would follow in their wake, for plunder, robbery and
pelf; and were guilty of many diabolical crimes too
heinous to mention. These were the fellows who
were designated, when the war closed, as scalawags
and "carpet-baggers," from the fact that all their
worldly effects consisted of an ancient hand-satchel, of
the black oilcloth variety, containing a paper collar,
a dirty shirt and a pair of rough army socks, slipped
from the clothes-line of some old friendly darkey
who had gone to the spring to procure for him a drink

of water. They were as much despised by the soldiers of the Federal army as by the people of the
South. The poor, ignorant negroes were not long in
finding out the infamously corrupt methods of this
despised and leprous set of poltroons.

The reconstruction period was fraught with great humiliation to the people of the South. The proud and
chivalric bearing of the Southerner had been crushed;
and many were so broken in spirits and in fortune
that they yielded to despondency and were consigned
to premature graves.

The new order of things was so at variance with
the time-honored customs, which formerly clustered
around their once happy homes, they were forced to
yield to the inevitable decree of fate and give up the
ghost.

Every city and town in the South was garrisoned
by Federal troops, and the work of reconstruction
moved slowly on. It was a vast and complicated
piece of machinery, with inexperienced hands at the
helm.

The ignorant negroes of the South were turned
adrift to assume all the responsibilities of their new-
made citizenship, and the carpet-bagger was at the
zenith of his earthly ambitions. He would never
let an occasion pass to impress upon the minds of
these poor ignorant creatures false notions of freedom.
In fact, the "bottom rail" was climbing rapidly toward the top. These wretches endeavored to impress
upon the minds of the negroes the strong feeling of
friendship they professed to entertain for the colored
race. They proved to be their worst enemies. They

held out the delusions to the negro that they were to
receive forty acres of land and a mule, and that the
government would furnish them with plenty of supplies; consequently they needn't do any more work.
These, with many other false and corrupt ideas, they
so turned the negroes' heads that they were fit sub-
jects for the lunatic asylum. Not being satisfied with
stuffing the negro brain with false notions, these pes-
tiferous dregs of humanity inaugurated a system by
which they could rob the negro of his hard earnings.
They established what was known as "The Freedman's Saving-banks," and in the fall of the year,
when the crops were being marketed they would in-
duce the negroes, by misrepresentations, to deposit
their small change with them, and when they had
about gathered in all his shekels, they would slide
out "for new fields and pastures green," leaving
Sambo to his own reflections. These fellows took to
politics as a duck to water, and would state to the
negroes that if they would support them for office
they would enact such laws as would place them in
possession of all the property held by their former
masters in the South; then they could live in ease
and idleness during the balance of their lives. Inflamed with this false and delusive idea of ease and
luxury the negroes in many settlements abandoned
the plantations and flocked to the towns, where they
could more readily communicate with their new-
found friends. They received no encouragement
from the soldiers, however, or from the Freedman's
Bureau, an institution established by the United
States Government for their protection. Political

gatherings finally became so annoying that the military was compelled to take the matter in hand and force them to return to the country and go to work. The minds of the negroes became so inflamed by false notions instilled by the carpet-bag element that it became necessary for the whites to take steps for their own protection.

Knowing that the negro, as a race, was very superstitious, and at the same time having no desire to do them an injury, they decided to play upon their credulity and organize what was known as the "Kuklux Klan." It sent up such a howl of indignation through the North and was magnified to such an extent that thousands believed it was an organization to exterminate the blacks. The politicians at the North took up the cue and waved on high the "bloody-shirt." The two combined managed to keep alive the embers of sectional strife, and ride into office on false representations of the Southern people, when in fact the "Kuklux Klan" were but a party of men, dressed in fantastic style, presenting a somewhat hideous appearance, simply to frighten the negro, as they had no desire to do him harm. It had the desired effect. The carpet-bagger would write back to his friends at the North (if he had any) the most exaggerated and blood-curdling accounts it was possible for his brain to invent, of the terrible outrages this mystic band was guilty of, without the slightest foundation in fact, for the statement. The troops stationed in the South understood the matter well, and not only did they, as a general thing, approve of the method, but in many instances joined the organization just for the sport of the thing.

The Southern people were disfranchised, and one of the leading features of reconstruction was to get them back into the Union. This was accomplished by requiring every one to march up and take an oath of allegiance to the United States Government, from which he had forsworn his fealty. Many were not allowed to take this oath; and this class (which con--isted of Confederate army officers above a certain rank and all who had held civil offices under the authority of the defunct government) were required to apply directly to the President of the United States for special pardon. This required much time and a vast consumption of "red-tape." Some even failed to get it then, unless they could show conclusively that their teeth were not made of crowbars and sharpened with the wrath of an avenging God; besides, that there were no horns protruding from the crowns of their heads.

The old soldiers rapidly took advantage of the proposition and returned to their allegiance, as they had no notion of remaining aliens in a country where they had sacrificed so much for constitutional rights. They returned to their shattered and desolate homes, and went to work with the same determined spirit which had characterized their conduct on so many bloody fields.

The first year after the surrender was a trying one for the Southern people. Most of them, especially the soldiers, were compelled to start life anew, with nothing to aid them but their own strong arms. It is said, however, that necessity is the mother of invention, so they hustled about and picked up, here and there, a few crippled horses and mules which had been abandoned by the armies and left by the wayside; these they recruited and made serve their purposes—in many instances they worked their milch cows. From the bark of trees they constructed traces, lines and collars; from rough pieces of wood they fabricated hames and plow-stocks. They forged their plows from such old pieces of scrap-iron as they could pick up here and there. With these improvised implements they succeeded in making a crop, paying very little attention to reconstruction, or the other methods and efforts to remodel the Union, feeling satisfied to remain at home.

The more intelligent negroes soon became disgusted with the false promises of the carpet-bagger, and gradually drifted back to the country, and others soon followed in their wake, where their former masters contracted with them at remunerative wages. They were once more happily back on the old plantation, with master and mistress to look after their welfare, and supply them with medicine, care, and dainties when sick. Many of the negroes were never allured away by the glitter of newly found freedom, but remained close to the old home, where the "'possum and the tater" luxuriated in profusion. Simple minded though they were, deep down in their sable breasts throbbed hearts as full of love and affection as ever pulsated beneath a white skin. The younger generation of whites in the South, who have sprung up since the war, will never know the love and ven-

eration felt by the old-time darkey for the inmates of
the "big house," as they called the dwelling-place of
the white family. It was here that the old black
mammy walked supreme, in all her queenly dignity,
regarded with all due deference to her exalted station,
by others of her race, and held in affectionate regard
by every member of the household, who consulted her
upon all matters connected with the nursery and the
culinary departments. She was always found by the
bedside of her sick master, mistress, and of the children; and her black face would lighten up with delight at each manifestation of a change for the better.
It was often that through the gentle care and nursing
of these faithful old darkeys the invalid was restored
to health. The picture is not overdrawn when it is
stated that never in the history of the world has such
unselfish devotion been surpassed as was evidenced by
these same "old family servants" of the South.
Many, many instances occurred during the war when
ladies and children were left for months on plantations, with hundreds of slaves upon them, who were
humble, devoted, and obedient to their every command; and who would have shed their last drop of
blood in defense of their master's interests and the
protection of his family. They had access to the "big
house" at all hours of the day and night; carried the
keys to the closets, smokehouse and cribs, and never
for a moment did the owners mistrust their loyalty
or the negroes betray the confidence reposed in them.
These facts are related that the attitude of the negroes,
towards the whites (and *rice versa*) of the South, during the long and bloody contest, may not be wholly

overlooked. They have earned a conspicuous place
in the history of the great war. The old-time darkey
is passing away; and rapidly is the civilization of
those times becoming extinct; and but few of the
old "uncles" and "aunties" are left. It is only now
and then that we see one hobbling about on a stick;
and these always, in a humble manner, address the
whites as "marster" or "missis." It speaks volumes for the great big heart of the Southern people,
that they never let one of these faithful old creatures
suffer, if in their power to relieve them. An appropriate and enduring monument should be erected,
somewhere in the Southern States, in commemora-
tion of their loyalty and devotion to the women and
children of the South, while our men were in the
field fighting to perpetuate their bondage. (Since
writing the above, I have learned that a monument
has been recently erected in memory of slaves faithful during the war, by a prominent citizen of South
Carolina, at his private expense.)

CHAPTER XXV.

THE BLOODY-SHIRT—WHO BUILT IT AND HOW—NOT THE SOLDIERS WHO HAD BEEN IN THE FRONT—LONGSTREET—MORALIZINGS.

Some of the chief actors in the great " Rebellion " were the first to lend their aid and devote their talents and energy in aiding to bring about a reconciliation between the two sections, North and South ; while there were others who took a small part in the great struggle and who were often interposing obstructions. Had it been left to the soldiers of the two armies, a settlement of the whole matter could have been had in twenty-four hours, or less time ; for they were willing to " clasp hands across the bloody chasm."

There was an element at the North that went into the war and made splendid soldiers—by *substitute*. These sought, for personal and political aggrandizement, to keep up the strife after the fighting had ended. Then there was an element at the South that had occupied some good bomb-proof positions while the boys were at the front. These were loudest in their denunciations of every effort to harmonize. These two disturbing factions rendered the work of reconstruction slow and tedious. There was a class of people in the South who, I regret to mention, but it must be written, were rampant secessionists at the start, and proclaimed that one Southerner could whip ten Yankees. These fellows, when the fight commenced, skulked the issue, and slid out of the country, taking up their abode in Nassau, Havana, or some other near-by foreign port, where they were engaged in speculating in contraband goods. These skulkers and dodgers returned after the war with fat purses; many of whom pushed themselves to the front for positions of honor, trust and emoluments, while the old soldier was forced to give way to these vampires who "sold their birthright for a mess of pottage;" and many of them and their children continue to enjoy the fortunes they obtained at the price of blood. These fellows used every effort to scotch the wheels of reconstruction, and threw every obstacle possible in the way of the old Confeds who were using their best efforts to reconcile the opposing factions. One who suffered most from their slanderous abuse, was that grand old hero, General James Longstreet. Thanks to an All-wise Providence, he has outlived their vile slanders; and his name will stand conspicuously bright on the roll of fame long after his traducers have passed from the memory of man. General Longstreet was second to no military chieftain in the armies of the South or North. When the war closed he yielded gracefully to the arbitrament of the sword. Having been reared and educated a soldier, he recognized, at a glance, that "Othello's occupation was gone," and it was his duty to submit to the dictates of the conquerer, and upon this hypothesis he not only lent his talent and bent all his lofty energies to further the ends of reconstruction, but set the example to his fellow soldiers, by joining hands with those he had so recently opposed in deadly conflict to bring about the desired end as proof of his sincerity and love of country. He accepted an appointment from his old friend and college fellow, General Grant, who was at the time President of the United States. He was made collector of the port of New Orleans, and afterwards minister to Turkey. These were generous and noble acts on the part of General Grant, and must ever stand conspicuous as evidencing the generous nobility of his character. Some denounced Longstreet as a traitor to the South; and not a few of the newspapers in the South were filled with vituperation and abuse of the old hero, whose shoe latches they were unworthy to loose. The editors of these papers possessed so limited an amount of brains they could not comprehend his grand and noble object. There was one class, however, that never, within the knowledge of the writer, allowed a word of censure to pass their lips; these were the battle-scarred heroes who helped to make the old warrior's name famous throughout the world.

It was the writer's good fortune to meet General Longstreet in New Orleans, shortly after he had assumed his position there. While in conversation with him, he related the relationship existing between the Commander-in-chief of the Federal armies and himself. They had been at West Point together, where a warm attachment had commenced and still existed. When the war broke out they chose opposite sides, and their legions frequently confronted each other in deadly conflict, but no feeling of personal animosity was engendered; but, on the contrary, a warm feeling of respect and friendship had always

existed between them.   Each had found in the other
a "foeman worthy of his steel."   General Longstreet
was not alone in the position he assumed at the close
of the war.   Quite a number of distinguished officers
of the Confederate army followed along the same line.
Their example, admonition and advice, went far toward healing the bleeding and lacerated wounds of the
South, and bringing together in friendly relationship
the people of the two sections, who had been engaged
for four long years in a bloody and fratricidal war.
The example of these men was but another evidence
of our advanced civilization; and the words of censure that fell from the lips of those who condemned
their actions, simply illustrated the fact that their
narrow, contracted minds could not see the way to a
peaceful and quiet adjustment of our differences.
Their course, however, has been vindicated by a fair-
minded and generous public.   More is due to the
efforts of such men to restore the Union than they
have ever been given credit for.   They never skulked
when duty called, but yielded an unreserved acqui-
escence to the results of the war.   They were not
like some others who had gained military distinction
in the armies of the South; when, in after years, their
brows were wreathed with political honors, they suc-
cumbed to the tempter Mammon, and betrayed the
trusts reposed in them, even in the legislative halls
of the Nation.

Reconstruction was an experiment.   Never before
had the country been called upon to solve so intricate
a problem.   That some great mistakes were made,

our wisest statesmen, North and South, have been forced to admit.

While it is not the object of the writer to enter into a detailed account of the dark days of reconstruction, at the same time there should be no hesitancy in proclaiming the fact that the most important factor in the reconciliation of the two sections, was the indomitable will and determination of the soldiers of both armies, after they returned to their homes. The soldiers of the South went to work with Spartan bravery to build up the waste places and recuperate their shattered fortunes. The soldiers of the North returned to their homes and various occupations, or to the South, captured some fair Southern lassie, and cast their fortunes with those whom, but a short while before, they had confronted in deadly battle. Now they met as brothers, and clasped each other's hands in friendly greeting, while other nations looked upon such scenes with astonishment, they having predicted that it would require several generations to eradicate the bitter feelings engendered by the war. Why was it so? They were Americans; of the same kith and kin, worshiped at the same shrine, drank from the same fountain, and were reared under the same flag! Their forefathers had stood side by side at Bunker Hill, Valley Forge, and Yorktown. Barefooted, thinly clad and suffering from hunger, they had crossed the Delaware with Washington, amid a driving storm of sleet and drifting ice! Later on, they had sent the haughty Packinham, with the flower of the British army, flying in dismay before the invincible hosts of Jackson at New Orleans; and still later they had stormed the heights of Chepultepec, and carried the Stars and Stripes in victory into the very " Halls of the Montezumas."   The descendants of such heroic ancestors could not long remain apart; their traditions were the same.   There had been a family quarrel and it was nobody's business but their own; it was all over, and they could sit down by each other's firesides and, in a friendly chat, recount the perils of the past.

CHAPTER XXVI.

IN NEW ORLEANS—THE MEXICAN BEAUTY—MY
FEDERAL FRIEND—THE COLUMBIAN LADY—THE
WOUNDED TENNESSEEAN LEFT IN COLUMBIA—
TRUTH STRANGER THAN FICTION—MARRIAGE.

Sometimes unaccountable events will follow in
such rapid succession that they often appear stranger
than fiction.

It was in the latter part of 1865, the writer was
passing along Canal street, in the city of New Orleans—one of the most picturesque thoroughfares in
the South, with its broad driveway densely shaded by
water-oaks, its sparkling fountains surrounded by
rare tropical plants; the towering monuments to distinguished soldiers and statesmen, presented to the
observer a picture in which nature and art so beau-
tifully blend that he was loath to leave the enraptur-
ing scene. The Federal army held uninterrupted
possession of New Orleans from its capture in 1862,
until the close of the war. There was no evidence
of demolition as was to be seen in most other cities
of the South; on the contrary, everything indicated
that the Federal officers had an eye to its preservation. Her sanitary condition had been so regulated
that not a case of yellow fever had developed while
the Federal troops were in possession.

The sun had just immersed her last rays beneath
the placid bosom of the " Father of Waters " as I approached the Clay monument—the pride of the citi-

zens of the Crescent City. I discovered a party of ladies and gentlemen standing at the base of the statue, gazing intently on the cold, inanimate features of the great statesman. The shades of evening were falling fast, and the city was but dimly lighted, but I thought I recognized one of the faces. It might appear discourteous to approach any nearer; enough, however, had been seen to trace the outlines of a beautiful female face and figure. It occurred to me that I had seen it before in my wanderings. The group soon withdrew and walked off down the street. I followed at a respectful distance, bent on locating the party. They soon entered a spacious dwelling in the residence portion of the street. Though the parlor was brilliantly illuminated, the heavy lace curtains at the windows obstructed the view of any one from without. So I took down the number and retired, determined to renew my inquiry the next day. I first interviewed a policeman whom I chanced to meet, but he, not being overburdened with intelligence, was not calculated to give much satisfaction, so I decided to sleep on it and renew my search the next day. By diligent inquiry I ascertained that the house had recently been taken by a wealthy Spaniard. I was somewhat perplexed as to the next best step to take. By slow degrees light began to break in upon my bewildered mind. Could it be possible that the lady in question was the friend I had met some years ago in Mexico, under such peculiar circumstances? I would make bold to ascertain by writing her a note, stating the circumstances, and asking her permission to call at any hour she might designate. It was not without some misgivings as to my conjectures being correct that I dispatched the note by one of Africa's sable sons, and the reply was soon received. A glance at the address at once revealed the fact that there was no mistake; I was cordially invited to call at my earliest convenience.

I consulted my wardrobe and rigged out in my best outfit, which, while not in the latest Parisian style, I thought would pass muster. When I was ushered into the drawing-room, I found the young lady seated at the piano. She had just been singing one of her native songs and her mind was, no doubt, wandering to her far-off sunny home. She arose and extended her hand in a warm and gentle greeting. After the usual salutations had been passed, our conversation was directed to matters pertaining to the past, present and future. She informed me, in her pure, native accent that our mutual friend, with whom I had parted four years ago, on the banks of the Rio Grande and last in North Carolina, would reach the city in a few days. This was exceedingly gratifying to me. I was quite anxious to see him before I took my departure for Texas, whither I was bound. Time had wrought some changes in my fair young friend, since I last saw her. She informed me that her father had removed his family to New Orleans, to remain during the winter, that they might escape the excitement then existing in Mexico. He had only determined upon this course after the surrender of the Confederate army.

She told me the day when her friend was to reach

the city, and I was the first to greet him upon his
arrival. He expressed no little astonishment at the
happy surprise, as he termed it. We drove to the
St. Charles Hotel, where rooms had been previously
engaged. There he briefly outlined his future purposes. It was the writer's intention to have left the
city the next day, but at the earnest solicitation of
my friend, who had come to claim the hand of the
fair young Mexican, I decided to remain until after
the happy event had been consummated, which would
be as soon as the necessary arrangements could be
made. It is said that "misfortunes never come single handed;" the same might be said, with equal
propriety, about surprises. It was indeed a surprise
and an agreeable one to meet my old friends at such
a place and at such a time; particularly as a terrible
war had been fought since meeting one of them.
But another surprise awaited me, which equally astonished me. My friend informed me that on his
way to New Orleans he had stopped over at a thriv-
ing town in middle Tennessee, where he had previously located a party in whom we were both interested. "Who do you suppose it was?" he asked.

"I have no conception," was my reply. "Why,
"in a cozy little cottage, just at the outskirts of the
"city, I found the wounded Confederate soldier whom
"you transferred from a hospital in Columbia, S. C.,
"to a private house which I guarded at your re-
"quest. Beside him stood the young lady into whose
"keeping you had consigned him. By her kind and
"gentle nursing he soon recovered. In the mean-

" time a warm mutual attachment had developed be-
" tween them.

" When the war closed he returned to the Pal-
" metto State and claimed the hand of this priceless
" jewel of his heart; and transplanted one of Colum-
" bia's fairest flowers to his beautiful home in Ten-
" nessee. There I found them in all the enjoyment of
" blissful wedded life. I was given a warm and cordial
" reception and entertained with genuine old Southern
" hospitality. I acquainted them with my errand to
" New Orleans, and they exacted from me a promise
" that I would stop on my return and make them a
" visit. They made many inquiries about you, and
" I regretted that I could give them no positive in-
' formation as to your whereabouts. I informed
" them, however, that you had come out of the war
" all right; also of our meeting after the surrender of
" Johnson's army."

About three years later, while passing through
Tennessee, the writer spent a day with the happy
couple. It was a delightful visit; and in addition to
being warmly welcomed by my war-time friends, I
was greeted by a bright, curly-headed, blue-eyed, little boy, the pride of the household—and he bore the
names of the writer and the gallant Federal officer
who protected the father and the mother on that fearful night in Columbia.

It took but a few days to make the necessary
arrangements for the wedding, which was a quiet
affair. Cards were issued to a limited number; our
friends in Tennessee were not overlooked. The
nuptials were celebrated at the home of the bride in

the presence of a few invited guests. The ceremony was after the beautiful ritual of the Roman Catholic Church. Following the congratulations an elegant repast was served. The bride, as she stood in her queenly attire beside the handsome and manly form of the groom, was the observed of all observers. The wreath of orange blossoms, in the form of a crescent, that so gracefully adorned her brow, presented a rich contrast to her raven locks as they fell in flowing ringlets on her well-rounded shoulders. The chain, studded with costly gems, which encircled her neck was eclipsed in brilliancy only by the soft, mellow flashes of her dark, Southern eyes. The whole affair, in all its appointments, bespoke the highest type of culture and refinement, without the slightest attempt at display or ostentation.

Agreeable to previous arrangements, the couple took their departure the next morning for a bridal tour to Europe. The groom had been granted leave of absence for a year, and he informed me they would spend most of the time in foreign lands. His credentials were such as to give them a passport into the first circles of the old world. Amid the waving of handkerchiefs and the well-wishes of friends, I saw them board one of the floating palaces which at that time plied between New Orleans and Memphis, Tenn.

Over thirty years have elapsed since this happy event took place; and the pair who were married in New Orleans, as well as the couple in Tennessee, are still living, and each of their unions has been blessed with a group of happy children. Colonel B. has a son who graduated with distinction at West

Point Military Academy, and at this time is a rising young officer in the United States Army.

Colonel —— experienced much hard service in the West for a long time after he returned from Europe, but of late years he has spent much of his time in looking after his wife's large estate in Mexico.

For good and substantial reasons the names of the parties who figured in these episodes have been withheld, but the reader is assured that the imagination has not been drawn upon; on the contrary, the narrative is one of simple facts.

CHAPTER XXVII.

DESTITUTION OF THE CONFEDERATES—CARPET-
BAG RULE—THE COURTS A TRAVESTY ON JUS-
TICE—THE COTTON TAX—ITS EFFECT—RECUP-
ERATION UNDER TRYING CIRCUMSTANCES—
LINCOLN'S WARNING—SHYLOCK FOR GOLD—IN-
TRIGUES OF THE MONEY KINGS—NATIONAL
BANKS—BREAKERS AHEAD.

The first year after the war witnessed a desperate
struggle on the part of the Southern people, especially
the old soldiers, hundreds of whom had been wounded,
were broken in health, and entirely unfit for manual
labor. These poor fellows were compelled to resort
to every character of expedient by which to gain a
living; and it required nerve, courage and sagacity to
meet the new order of things and overcome the obstacles that beset their pathway.

The labor of the country was sadly demoralized.
The Carpet-bagger held full sway. The country was
under martial law. People were every day being
arrested and brought before a "shoulder-strap tribunal" on trumped-up charges, generally convicted and
fined according to their ability to pay, which fines
would go toward replenishing the exchequer of some
irresponsible official.

Their burdens were still further augmented by the
imposition of a revenue tax on every pound of cotton
raised. This unjust and arbitrary tax was in violation of the letter and spirit of the constitution of
the United States, an almost unknown authority at

that time, by the satraps who dispensed the governmental affairs of the South. This tax was collected by requiring all producers of cotton to purchase brass tags and to place one on every bale of cotton before going to market. Each bale was diligently scrutinized by a government official, and if one was found not to have this precious little jewel attached to it, it was at once confiscated, and the owner was left without any redress.

The burden of this tax fell heavily upon the " brother in black," the very element the government had taken under its fostering care. Sambo would chafe and champ the bit for awhile, but to no purpose; the tax had to come. When the tax, with half the expense for making the crop, and the time the darkey had lost in attending political meetings and military drills had been deducted from his part, he would find himself "non est in swampo," which, translated, means that Cuffy would find himself minus the necessary " wherewith" to purchase his " Christmas tricks," and left with the only alternative to enter into a new contract for another year that he might obtain food.

Cotton, for several years after the war, commanded a good price in the markets of the world, which enabled the people of the South, notwithstanding the many obstacles thrown in their way, to improve their condition. They continued to push ahead, and evidences of thrift and prosperity were to be seen on every hand. The outside world looked with wonder and astonishment upon the rapid strides they were making in recovering from the effects of a long and devastating war. This was much more of a surprise

when they realized the fact that all wars, to a greater
or less extent, blunt the industrial, moral and religious sensibilities, and open wide the doors of almost
every vice. While this may be true of a people low
in the scale of human development, it could not be
applied to the high moral and social culture of the
element that composed the armies of the South. True
to their traditions, the Southern people re-established
their schools and threw wide their doors of public
worship. Homes were being repaired and new ones
constructed. Thousands who never owned a foot of
land before bought farms and paid for them. Money
was plenty, and all kinds of labor was receiving remunerative wages. Mechanical and agricultural products commanded good prices. There were no enforced idlers in the land; all could find employment
who had a disposition to work. Sectional feeling
was gradually dying out, and the people of the South
were once more on the broad road to happiness and
prosperity. There was a currency circulation of over
$50 per capita, principally of paper money issued by the
government, known as " greenbacks," and was a legal
tender for the payment of all debts, public and private.
There was but a small amount of specie in circulation, but the masses of the people prospered without
it. This happy state of affairs was not long des-
tined to continue. While the country was making
rapid strides forward, that green-eyed monster, Shylock, was plotting a dark and infamous conspiracy
to rob and plunder the people. He could see nothing but gold, gold, gold! which was lying idle in
his vaults, and which must be made the standard, or

redemption money. In order to carry out his nefarious scheme of plunder, Congress was so manipu-
lated as to pass what was known as the " exception
clause," which required all duties on imports and
interest on the public debt should be paid in coin.
This act created a demand for Shylock's hoarded
gold and lessened the value of greenbacks, which reduced the wages of every laboring man, woman and
child in the country, and forced the soldier who had
carried the flag of his country to victory and made
possible an indissoluble Union to take for his services
a depreciated currency, while the robber barons of
Europe and Wall Street filled their coffers with
blood-money, gold. By this act the government was
made to assume the rôle of robber that others might
become rich. From the moment of the passage of
this act property of all kinds commenced to de-
preciate in value. Not only was the South made to
suffer by this diabolical outrage, but the great
Northwest was plunged into the vortex of almost
ruin. The depreciation was so slight at first that
it was some time before the people began to realize
its effects.

The next villainous scheme inaugurated by the
money sharks for robbing the people, was the passage
by Congress of the National Bank Act. This followed close upon the " exception clause," as a necessary consequence.

I will not discuss the workings of this fraudulent
system, but for the benefit of any who may entertain
a doubt of its being the deliberate purpose of the act

to swindle and rob the people, a private circular is here given, which was sent out by the secretary of the " Bankers' Association," which reads as follows:

" DEAR SIR:—It is advisable to do all in your " power to sustain such daily and prominent weekly " newspapers, especially the *agricultural* and *religious* " press, as will oppose the issuing of greenback paper " money; and that you withhold patronage or favors " from all applicants who are unwilling to oppose the " government issue of money.

" Let the government issue the *coin* and the *banks* " issue the *paper money* of the country; then we can " better protect each other. To repeal the law creat-" ing national banks and to restore to circulation the " government issue of money, will be to provide the " people with moneys, and will, therefore, seriously " affect your individual profits as banker and lender. " See your member of Congress at once, and engage " him to support our interest, that we may control "legislation.   Signed by the Secretary,

                              " JAS. BUELL.."

This precious document should be framed and hung in a conspicuous place in the house of every farmer and laboring man in the land, where he can read his doom in every line. The greenback currency was the money of the people. It was issued in such convenient sums as would meet all business transactions; and its destruction was but a link in the system of legalized robbery. To go on and note the great number of schemes employed by the money gods of Europe, and their satellites in America, to rob the people, would require a volume.

It required only a few years after the war closed for Shylock to get the machinery of " contraction " in good working order. By tightening the "thumb-screws" by slow degrees he could gradually bring the masses to a state of vassalage. To show how this grinding process worked with the farmers of the South a statement is here given, made by a Georgia editor :

" In 1868 there was about $40 per capita of money
" in circulation. Cotton was about 30 cents a pound.
" The farmer tl en put a 500-pound bale of cotton on
" his wagon, took it to town and sold it. Then he
" Paid taxes $40 00
" Bought a cooking-stove for 30 00
" A suit of clothes for 15 00
" One hundred pounds of meat for.......... 18 00
" One barrel of flour for.................. 12 00
" and went home with $35 in his pocket. In 1887
" there was about $5 per capita of money in circula-
" tion ; this same farmer put a 500-pound bale of cot-
" ton on his wagon, went to town and sold it, paid
" $40 taxes, got discouraged, went to the saloon, spent
" the remainder, and went home dead broke and
" drunk.

" In the same proportion was the farmer of the
" West affected. In the short space of nineteen years
" over $1,200,000,000 of the people's money had been
" withdrawn from circulation. The loss in business
" failures cannot be estimated; strikes were frequent;
" the country was rapidly becoming run over with
" tramps."

Things have been going on from bad to worse until now, the year of our Lord 1896, it is beyond the power of numbers to compute the depreciation of every species of property, and unless the people arise

in their might and throttle the red-handed monster, Corruption, our boasted Republic, for the preservation of which so much blood and treasure has been expended, will be forever lost.   If the advice and admonition of some of our wisest statesmen in the past had been heeded, the great calamity which now threatens to prostrate our fair land at the feet of a despotic money power, might have been averted.   It is not that the people have not had due and timely warning of the approach of the danger which threatens to wreck their financial ship.   As far back as the middle of the present century the distinguished philosopher and patriot, Sir John Lubbock, of England, declared: " There is likely an effort to be made by " the capital class to fasten upon the world a rule " through their wealth, and by means of reduced " wages place the masses upon a footing more degrad- " ing than has ever been known in history."   The spirit of the money-worshippers seems to be rapidly developing in this direction.

A few years later the revered statesman and martyred President, Abraham Lincoln, reiterated the same sentiment in his message to Congress in 1861, which is recorded in Barratt's " Life of Lincoln," pages 309 and 310.

This timely warning does not appear in histories of later date: " Monarchy itself is sometimes hinted as " a possible refuge from the power of the people.   In " my present position I could scarcely be justified " were I to omit raising a warning voice against the " approach of returning despotism.   There is one " point to which I ask brief attention.   It is the effort "to place capital on an equal footing with, if not "above labor in the structure of government. . . . "Let them beware of surrendering a political power "which they already have, and which, if surrendered, "will surely be used to close the door of advance- "ment against such as they, and to fix new disabil- "ities and burdens upon them until their liberty shall "be lost." These are honest words of warning, ema- nating from a loyal heart, whose every pulsation was in sympathy with the great masses of the people.

Again we have a warning voice from the same ex- alted source. It was near the close of the war that Mr. Lincoln penned the following eloquent words in reply to a letter from a friend in Illinois: "Yes, we "may all congratulate ourselves that this cruel war is "nearing a close. It has cost a vast amount of blood "and treasure. The best blood of the flower of our "American youth has been freely offered upon our "country's altar that the Nation might live. It has "indeed been a trying hour for the Republic; but I "see in the near future a crisis approaching. It un- "nerves me and causes me to tremble for the safety "of my country. As a result of the war corporations "have been enthroned, and an era of corruption in "high places will follow, and the money power of the "country will endeavor to prolong its reign by work- "ing upon the prejudices of the people until all wealth "is aggregated into a few hands, and the Republic is "destroyed. I feel at this moment more anxiety for "the safety of my country than ever before, even in "the midst of the war. God grant that my suspicions "may prove to be groundless. History proves that

" nothing is so disastrous to nations as the enactment
" of laws which favor the few at the expense of the
" many."

The penetrating gaze of this sagacious statesman
pierced the veil of the future and saw the handwriting
on the wall.   His pathetic words made no impression
upon Shylock, whose heart is as cold as a Norwegian
iceberg, and who stands ready, with his vulture-like
beak, to pluck the bones of a dead republic.

But one way remains by which the " Old Ship of
State" can become extricated from her perilous condition, and once more be launched upon the broad ocean
of prosperity, freighted with a happy and prosperous
people.   Let the old veterans of both armies fall into
line, with the " Stars and Stripes" waving over their
heads, march to the polls; and there, with a perfect
cyclone of ballots, hurl from power the bloated min-
ions of corruption—these legalized robbers, who, with
cunning hand, scheming brain, and blackened souls,
are plotting the overthrow of the republic, and upon
the sacred altar of Liberty once more establish a government *of the people, by the people and for the people!*
When this shall have been consummated, the old
soldiers can unfurl their banners to the breeze and
join in the beautiful refrain of the "Blue and the
Gray," which was written by one of the South's most
gifted daughters, Frances Miles Finch. She was
seized by the inspiration of the hour, when at the
decoration of the soldier's graves at Columbus, Miss.

A few years since, the ladies of that beautiful inland city showed themselves impartial in the floral
offerings made to the memory of the dead by strew-

ing flowers alike on the graves of the **Confederate**
and of the Federal soldiers.

"By the flow of the inland river,
　Whence the fleets of iron have fled,
Where the blades of the grave-grass quiver,
　Asleep are the ranks of the dead ;
　　Under the sod and the dew,
　　　Waiting the judgment day;
　　Under the one, the Blue;
　　　Under the other, the Gray.

"These in the robings of glory,
　Those in the gloom of defeat ;
All with the battle-blood gory,
　In the dusk of eternity meet ;
　　Under the sod and the dew,
　　　Waiting the judgment day;
　　Under the laurel, the Blue;
　　　Under the willow, the Gray.

" From the silence of sorrowful hours,
　The desolate mourners go,
Lovingly laden with flowers,
　Alike for the friend and the foe ;
　　Under the sod and the dew,
　　　Waiting the judgment day ;
　　Under the roses, the Blue ;
　　　Under the lilies, the Gray.

" So with an equal splendor,
　The morning sun-rays fall,
With a touch impartially tender,
　On the blossoms blooming for all ;
　　Under the sod and the dew,
　　　Waiting the judgment day ;
　　Broidered with gold, the Blue ;
　　　Mellowed with gold, the Gray.

" So when the summer calleth,
　On forest and field of grain,
With an equal murmur falleth
　The cooling drops of the rain ;

Under the sod and the dew,
  Waiting the judgment day;
Wet with the rain, the Blue;
  Wet with the rain, the Gray.

"Sadly, but not with upbraiding,
  The generous deed was done;
In the storm of the years that are fading,
  No braver battle was won;
      Under the sod and the dew,
        Waiting the judgment day;
      Under the blossoms, the Blue;
        Under the garlands, the Gray.

" No more shall the war-cry sever,
  Or the winding rivers be red;
They banish our anger forever,
  When they laurel the graves of our dead;
      Under the sod and the dew,
        Waiting the judgment day;
      Love and tears for the Blue;
        Tears and love for the Gray."

APPENDIX.

JACK WILLS'S PETITION TO CONGRESS FOR AMNESTY.

During the days of Reconstruction, Jack Wills's petition for pardon attracted widespread attention. Although this remarkable document possesses a degree of merit far beyond many productions which have given world-wide fame, it has well-nigh faded from the public mind.

Jack's petition was read in Congress by Proctor Knott, in that distinguished statesman's inimitable style, and his motion that the pardon be granted, was seconded by that fiery Radical leader, General B. F. Butler.

The prayer for pardon was not only granted, but Jack's more fervent petition for a good, fat office was immediately answered, and he was given an appointment as "Register in Bankruptcy" for one of the mountain districts of Kentucky.

Proctor Knott and James B. Beck represented Kentucky in the United States Senate, when the following petition was made :

"Dear Knott: I thought, as I had time,
I'd write to you and Beck in rhyme,
To let you know that I am well,
A span's length yet, or more, from hell.
I also send petition signed
By loyal men, who were so kind
As to indorse and recommend
For clemency, your wayward friend.

Please push it through, and thus relieve
A rebel who passed sins doth grieve;
And you may tell each friendly Rad
That though I was a rebel bad,
My penitence is deep and true,
More than I dare express to you.
When Jeptha, judge of Israel's God,
To drown his foes in their own blood,
He made a vow he 'hadn't orter,'
And thereby lost his only daughter;
This now I'm sure old Jep repented
Until he felt almost demented.
If all of Holy Writ is true,
Old Pharaoh did the Jews pursue
With numerous hosts, intent on slaughter,
Until he got neck-deep in water;
With penitence, no doubt profound,
His soul was filled, before he drowned.
And thousands evil ways have tried,
Who felt repentance e'er they died;
But few have felt the deep contrition
As he who sends you this petition.
Some for their crimes get thrown in prison,
And some get ropes around their 'wizen';
Some after death are sent to hell;
All these can bear their fates quite well;
But he who with a gory hand,
Stirs up rebellion in the land,
'Gainst the best government under the sun,
And fails in his purpose, is forever undone.
No prison for him! Let no gallows be built!
The red ocean of hell is too mild for his guilt!
That pit of perdition, where the devil and his kith
Are weeping and wailing and gnashing their teeth,
Is too full of pleasure.   Let's invent some new plan
To punish and torture this rebellious clan!
Thus our law-makers said and with cruel intendment,
Went to work and concocted the Fourteenth Amendment.
A man can stand being hung or put in jail,
Face the guillotine too, without turning pale,
And pleasantly travel the pathway to hell
And plunge in as though without fear he fell.

But just think, my dear Proc, and you are no novice,
How a Kentuckian feels when he can't hold office!
Old Spain's inquisition, and the racks they applied
To torture mankind, may thrice be multiplied;
Then add gallows and jails, and the fortunes of hell
And the figures you get, begin scarcely to tell
The miseries of him whose seal of descendment
Is laid down by law in the Fourteenth Amendment.
Not that he cares much for the Yankee blood spilt,
Or for the ones he has wounded or those he has kilt,
But his cup of misery is full to the brim
When the holding of office is denied unto him.
Remorse and repentance express but contentment
When compared with the rule in this Fourteenth Amend-
    ment.
Why, it's bad enough, Proc, when he can't get elected;
It makes him feel sorry, repentant, dejected;
But to say he shan't run; why, ye gods, what contrition
Fills up a man's heart in this awful condition!
Such a condition is mine, and it worries me more
And pierces my soul to my heart's very core;
And I am sure when your friends can see how I'm grieved
They'll hurry up the cakes and get me relieved.
O, my country, my country! how I'd like to serve it
In some good, fat office, for I know I deserve it.
You may tell your friends, too, I'll remember in prayer,
Those who in relieving your friend, shall take a share,
And I'll here give a specimen prayer by the way,
For fear they may think I don't know how to pray:
Thou Ruler of both good and bad,
Look down and bless each friendly Rad
Who hastens forward with agility
To free Jack Wills of disability.
May pleasure on his pathway shine,
May he for office never pine.
May he never know defeat
(Unless some Reb can get his seat);
May he live a thousand years,
His eyes be never wet with tears,
Except it be with tears of joy,
Of pleasure mixed with no alloy,
And spend his days in sweet contentment,
Free from the d—ned Fourteenth Amendment!"

THE CONQUERED BANNER.

BY FATHER ABRAM J. RYAN, THE POET-PRIEST OF THE
SOUTH.

Furl that banner, for 'tis weary,
Round its staff 'tis drooping dreary,
   Furl it, fold it, it is best;
For there's not a man to wave it,
And there's not a sword to save it,
And there's not one left to lave it
In the blood which heroes gave it—
And its foes now scorn and brave it—
   Furl it, hide it, let it rest.

Take that banner down—'tis tattered,
Broken is its staff and shattered,
And the valiant hosts are scattered
   Over whom it floated high.
Oh! 'tis hard for us to fold it,
Hard to think there's none to hold it,
Hard that those who once unrolled it,
   Now must furl it with a sigh.

Furl that banner, furl it sadly—
Once ten thousand hailed it gladly,
And ten thousands wildly, madly,
   Swore it should forever wave;
Swore that foeman's sword could never
Hearts like theirs entwined, dissever,
Till that flag would float forever
   O'er their freedom or their grave!

Furl it, for the hands that grasped it,
And the hands that fondly clasped it,
   Cold and dead are lying low;
And the banner, it is trailing,
While around it sounds the wailing
   Of its people in their woe.

For, though conquered, they adore it,
Love the cold dead hands that bore it,
Weep for those who fell before it,
Pardon those who trailed and tore it,
And oh! wildly they deplore it,
   Now to furl and fold it so.

Furl that banner; true, 'tis gory,
Yet 'tis wreathed around with glory
And 'twill live in song and story,
  Though its folds are in the dust;
For its fame on brightest pages,
Penned by poets and by sages,
Shall go sounding down the ages,
Furl its folds though now we must.
Furl that banner, softly, slowly,
Treat it gently, it is holy—
  For it droops above the dead;
Touch it not, unfold it never,
Let it droop there, *furled* forever,
  For its people's *hopes* are dead."

ALL QUIET ALONG THE POTOMAC TO-NIGHT.

BY LAMAR FONTAIN, SECOND VIRGINIA CAVALRY.

All quiet along the Potomac to-night,
 Except here and there a stray picket
Is shot, as he walks on his beat to and fro,
 By a rifleman hid in the thicket.
'Tis nothing—a private or two now and then
 Will not count in the news of the battle;
Not an officer lost, only one of the men
 Moaning out, all alone, the death-rattle.

All quiet along the Potomac to-night,
 Where the soldiers lie peacefully dreaming;
Their tents, in the rays of the clear autumn moon,
 Or the light of the watch-fires gleaming.
A tremulous sigh, as the gentle night wind
 Through the forest leaves slowly is creeping,
While the stars up above, with their glittering eyes,
 Keep guard, for the army is sleeping.

There is only the sound of the lone sentry's tread,
 As he tramps from the rock to the fountain;
And thinks of the two on the low trundle-bed,
 Far away in the cot on the mountain.

His musket falls slack; his face, dark and grim,
  Grows gentle with memories tender,
As he mutters a prayer for his children asleep;
  For their mother—may Heaven defend her!

The moon seems to shine as brightly as then,
  That night, when the love, yet unspoken,
Leaped up to his lips, and when low-murmured vows
  Were pledged, to be ever unbroken.
Then drawing his sleeve roughly over his eyes,
  He dashes off tears that are welling;
And gathers his gun close up to its place
  As if to keep down the heart's swelling.

He passes the fountain, the blasted pine-tree,
  The footstep is lagging and weary;
Yet onward he goes through the broad belt of light
  Toward the shades of the forest so dreary.
Hark! Was it the night wind that rustled the leaves?
  Was it moonlight so wondrously flashing?
It looked like a rifle—Ah! Mary, good-bye!
  And his life-blood is ebbing and splashing.

"All quiet along the Potomac to-night!"
  No sound save the rush of the river;
While soft falls the dew on the face of the dead,
  And the picket's off duty forever!

THE NINTH OF APRIL, 1865.

BY PERCY GREG,

*Of Dorster Hall, Surry, England, author of Greg's History
of the United States.*

It is a Nation's death-cry—yes, the agony is past!
The stoutest race that ever fought, to-day has fought its
  last.
Aye! start and shudder, well thou may'st;
Well veil thy weeping eyes:
England! may God forgive thy part—man cannot but
  despise!

Aye! shudder at that cry that speaks the South's supreme
  despair:
Those that could save and saved'st not; that would, yet
  did not dare:
Thou that had'st might to aid the right and heart to brook
  the wrong;
Weak words of comfort for the weak and strong hands to
  help the strong.
That land, the garden of thy wealth, one haggard waste
  appears—
The ashes of her sunny homes are slaked in patriot tears!
Tears for the slain who died in vain for freedom, on the
  field;
Tears, tears of bitter anguish still for those who live to
  yield.
The cannon of his country pealed Stewart's funeral knell;
His soldiers' cheers rang in his ears as Stonewall Jackson
  fell;   :
Onward o'er gallant Ashby's grave swept war's successful
  tide,
And Southern hopes were living yet, when Polk and Mor-
  gan died.
But he, the leader, on whose words the captains loved to
  wait;
The noblest, bravest, best of all, hath found a harder fate;
Unscathed by shot and steel, he passed o'er many a des-
  perate field :
Oh, God! that he hath lived so long and only lived to
  yield!   ꞇ
Along the war-worn, wasted ranks that loved him to the
  last,
With saddened face and weary pace, the vanquished chief-
  tain passed;
Their own hard lot the men forgot, they felt what his
  must be;
What thought, in that dark hour, must wring the heart of
  General Lee.
The manly cheek with tears was wet, the stately head was
  bowed,
As breaking from their shattered ranks, around his steed
  they crowd;

"I did the best for you." 'Twas all those trembling lips
  could say:
Ah! happy those whom death hath spared the anguish of
  to-day.
Weep on, Virginia! weep these lives given to thy cause in
  vain,
The sons who live to wear once more the Union's galling
  chain;
The homes whose light is quenched for aye—the graves
  without a stone—
The folded flag—the broken sword—the hope forever flown!
Yet raise thy head, fair land, thy dead died bravely for the
  right:
The folded flag is stainless still—the broken sword is bright;
No blot on thy record's found; no treason soils thy fame!
Weep thou thy dead, with covered head, we mourn our
  England's shame!

THE BIVOUAC OF THE DEAD.

BY THEODORE O'HARA.

The muffled drum's sad roll has beat
    The soldier's last tattoo;
No more on life's parade shall meet
    That brave and fallen few.
On Fame's eternal camping-ground
    Their silent tents are spread,
And Glory guards, with solemn round,
    The bivouac of the dead.

No rumor of the foe's advance
    Now swells upon the wind;
No troubled thought at midnight hour
    Of loved ones left behind;
No vision of the morrow's strife
    The warrior's dream alarms,
No braying horn or screaming fife
    At dawn shall call to arms.

Their shivered swords are red with rust,
　Their plumed heads are bowed,
Their haughty banner, trailed in dust,
　Is now their martial shroud;
And plenteous funeral tears have washed
　The red stains from each brow,
And the proud forms, by battle gashed,
　Are free from anguish now.

The neighing troop, the flashing blade,
　The bugle's stirring blast,
The charge, the dreadful cannonade,
　The din and shout are past;
Nor war's wild note, nor glory's peal
　Shall thrill with fierce delight
Those breasts that never more may feel
　The rapture of the fight.

Like the fierce northern hurricane
　That sweeps his great plateau,
Flushed with the triumph yet to gain,
　Came down the serried foe;
Who heard the thunder of the fray
　Break o'er the field beneath,
Knew well the watchword of that day
　Was victory or death.

Full many a norther's breath has swept
　O'er Angostura's plain,
And long the pitying sky has wept
　Above its moldered slain.
The raven's scream, or eaglet's flight,
　Or shepherd's pensive lay,
Alone now wake each solemn height
　That frowned o'er that dread fray.

Sons of the dark and bloody ground,
　Ye must not slumber there,
Where stranger steps and tongues resound
　Along the heedless air;
Your own proud land's heroic soil
　Shall be your fitter grave;
She claims from war its richest spoil--
　The ashes of her brave.

Thus, 'neath their parent turf they rest,
   Far from the gory field,
Borne to a Spartan mother's breast,
   On many a bloody shield.
The sunshine of their native sky
   Smiles sadly on them here,
And kindred eyes and hearts watch by
   The heroes' sepulcher.

Rest on, embalmed and sainted dead,
   Dear as the blood ye gave!
No impious footsteps here shall tread
   The herbage of your grave;
Nor shall your glory be forgot
   While Fame her record keeps,
Or Honor points the hallowed spot
   Where Valor proudly sleeps.

Yon marble minstrel's voiceless stone
   In deathless song shall tell,
When many a vanished year hath flown,
   The story how he fell;
Nor wreck, nor change, nor winter's blight,
   Nor Time's remorseless doom,
Can dim one ray of holy light
   That gilds your glorious tomb.

MORGAN'S WAR SONG.

Ye sons of the South, take your weapons in hand!
For the foot of the foe hath insulted your land.
      Sound, sound the loud alarm!
      Arise, arise and arm!

Let the hand of each freeman grasp the sword to maintain
Those rights, once lost, he can never regain!
Gather fast 'neath our flag, for 'tis God's own decree
That its folds shall still float o'er a land that is free!

See ye not those strange clouds which now darken the sky?
Hear ye not that stern thunder now bursting so nigh?
      Shout, shout your battle-cry!
      Win, win this fight or die!

To your country devote every life that she gave;
Let the land they invade give the enemy their grave.
　　　　Shout, shout your battle-cry!
　　　　Win, win this fight or die!

On our hearts and our cause and our God, we rely;
And a nation shall rise, or a people shall die!
　　　　Form, form the serried line!
　　　　Advance the proud ensign!

What our fathers achieved our own valor can keep;
And we'll save our fair land, or we'll sleep our last sleep
　　　　Form, form the serried line!
　　　　Advance the proud ensign!

Kentucky, Kentucky! can you suffer the sight
Of your sisters insulted; your friends in the fight!
　　　　Awake! be free again!
　　　　O, break the tyrant's chains!

Sure the sword you once drew but to strike for the right;
From the homes of your fathers drive the vandals in flight
　　　　Awake! be free again!
　　　　O, break the tyrant's chain!

A RELIC OF THE WAR RETURNED.

It will be remembered that, on the night of General Morgan's marriage, he started on a raid into Kentucky; that we first met the Federals at Bardstown, and, after a hard fight, captured the garrison, of over one thousand men; that we then moved rapidly on to Muldraugh's Hill, on the Louisville and Nashville railroad, where there was an important trestle guarded by four hundred and eighty of the Seventy-first Indiana regiment, which was also captured and the trestle burned. It was at this last surrender that I received a sword, which I used during the rest of the war. That it saw service is attested by its broken and battered scabbard.

After the war I married, and the old sword was put in a lumber-room, where it remained until the curiosity of my oldest boy prompted an investigation of the contents of the room.

Finding this rusty, old sword, he undertook to scour off the rust; in doing so he discovered some lettering, and, not being able to read it, brought the sword to me to tell him what it was. Then, for the first time, I noticed the inscription. I immediately wrote to the postmaster at Perrysville, not knowing Lieutenant Sinks's address, with the following result:

(From the Indianapolis *Journal*, August 15, 1883.)

THE BLUE AND THE GRAY.

A Reminiscence of the Late War—One of John Morgan's Soldiers, who Captured a Sword from a Perrysville Man, Now Proposes to Return it to the Owner—A Southern Soldier's Friendly Feeling for the Boys who Wore the Blue.

The following letters will fully explain themselves, and remind many of our readers of a little incident that occurred during the late war:

PERRYSVILLE, July 20th, 1883.

S. B. Davis:

SIR :—The following is a copy of a letter just received by me, which might be of interest to the readers of the *Hoosier*. If you think proper, you may publish it.   SMITH RABB.

Madison, Morgan County, Ga.,
July 15th, 1883.

To the Postmaster of Perrysville, Ind. :

DEAR SIR:—I have in my possession an old war relic, which is a sword, with the following inscription on the sheath :

"J. M. SINKS,
71st. Reg.,
Ind. Vol.
Presented by the citizens of Perrysville."

This sword was captured in Kentucky. I was an officer in General John Morgan's command. Thinking that this relic might be of interest to the gentleman to whom it was presented, or if dead, to some friends, I have thought it no more than right and just, as also due from one soldier to another, to make an effort to return it.

Those stirring times of long ago are past, and I would grasp the hand of one who fought against me with the same warmth that I would greet one of my old companions in arms.

If you will make the contents of this communication known to the parties interested, I will take pleasure in forwarding the same by express to the owner.

Very respectfully,
J. P. AUSTIN,
Madison, Morgan County, Ga.

Mr. J. M. Sinks resides in Indianapolis, and I send him the original letter, and if he does not see proper to send for the sword we will send for it, as I was one of the men that helped to buy it for him.

S. RABB.

A RELIC OF THE WAR.

While the encampment is in progress and Indianapolis is resplendent with appropriate military decorations and patriotic emblems, reminiscences of the days when "the boys were marching" are of more than usual interest. Lieutenant J. M. Sinks, of the old Seventy-first Indiana, received a relic of his soldiering days yesterday, which was doubly welcome, because of its unexpectedness. In the battle of Muldrough's Hill, he was one of a detail of four hundred and eighty members of the regiment who were detailed to guard a bridge. The enemy came down upon them with unexpected force, and captured the entire command. Shortly before this the citizens of Perrysville had presented to each of the officers of the regiment a handsome sword and other accoutrements, and Lieutenant Sinks's was taken from him. From that day until yesterday he heard nothing of it, but yesterday morning he received an express package containing the weapon, accompanied by the following letter of explanation:

"I this day forward this relic to its rightful owner. The trappings are all lost. The end of the scabbard was broken off by a shot in the battle of Atlanta. The sword has been in an out-of-the-way place for a long time. It is no more than right, as also due from one soldier to another, to return it. Those stirring times of long ago are past, and I would grasp the hand of one who fought against me with the same warmth that I would greet one of my old companions in arms. I hope you will receive the sword all right, and hope that it may never be drawn only in defense of that flag which it is the duty of every good citizen to love, honor and respect. I regret that I cannot attend your encampment, but it is impossible.

"J. P. Austin, Madison, Ga."